Andrew Culver

Oswald's Odyssey: Two Hours in Dallas

ISBN 9781519019196

Introduction

This timeline covers the two-hour period before Kennedy was assassinated up to the point that Lee Harvey Oswald was arrested at the Texas Theater, from noon to 2:00 on November 22, 1963. I compiled the timeline because I wanted to know exactly what happened, from minute to minute, according to all the relevant witnesses. I couldn't find exactly what I was looking for in the assassination literature, so I began to do my own research. I had no idea the timeline would grow to the size that it did.

What I couldn't find anywhere else, even in Mary Ferrell's excellent chronologies, was a focus on what the witnesses said that they saw – and *when* they made their testimonies. I wanted to know what witnesses said the day of the assassination, and what they said in the weeks and months following the assassination. I wanted to see how stories were changed, how they stayed consistent, and how they became absorbed into the narrative of the Warren Report.

The timeline includes sources for every statement, and I have tried to tell the reader when and in what context each testimony was given. Obviously the witnesses' memories did not improve with time, and when the Warren Commission interviewed the subjects, it was at least three months after November 22nd (the first interviews began on February 3rd of 1964). The witnesses had been subjected to a media blitz that told them repeatedly that Oswald had acted alone. I do not know what other kinds of pressure they were subjected to.

Warren Reynolds, who witnessed J.D. Tippit's killer leaving the crime scene, was shot in the head in January, two days after telling the FBI that he could not definitely identify the killer. He survived and positively identified Oswald as Tippit's killer when the Warren Commission interviewed him. His memory seemed to have improved after the gunshot to the head. Many witnesses were simply not called to the Commission, and many others were interviewed in such a way that any statements that deviated from the "lone nut theory" were ignored or brushed aside.

I view the reliability of evidence in a sliding scale, from most to least reliable:

1) The Dallas Police dispatches, which were recorded in real time as the police were reacting to the assassination (later transcribed by the Dallas PD for the Warren Commission);

2) The testimonies collected on the 22nd and 23rd, either live on the radio or by the FBI or police;

3) The testimonies collected in the weeks following the assassination;

4) The testimonies collected by the Warren Commission in their investigation, between February and September of 1964;

5) The books written in the years following the assassination, drawing from eyewitness accounts and interviews.

An article by Greg Miller in *Smithsonian Magazine* (May 2010) described some recent research on the way memory works. A 2003 study of 569 New York college students found that, just seven weeks after the attacks of 9/11, 73% of the students incorrectly remembered the event, believing that they had witnessed the first tower falling live on television (it wasn't broadcast live). Karim Nader, a neuroscientist at McGill University, has studied the way that people remember traumatic or important events, and believes that the act of remembering, or describing the event, may change the memory itself. These memories become more inaccurate over time. We should keep this in mind when studying the assassination.

A few insights have emerged from this project. There is the sense of a narrative being aggressively pushed on the public, based on a complex mass of eyewitness statements. This "official" narrative began immediately after the assassination, on the 22nd of November. It was solidified unofficially in the media in the months following the assassination, and officially by Warren Commission, who presented this narrative to the public as a closed case almost a year after the event.

The official story is known to most Americans – a communist sympathizer named Lee Harvey Oswald killed Kennedy by shooting him with three bullets from the 6th floor of the Texas School Book Depository, and then in his escape, he shot and killed a police officer named J.D. Tippit, and was captured in a movie theater. Much of the case against Oswald was assembled as early as November 30, just eight days after the assassination, as we can see in the FBI's massive Gemberling Report (Commission Document 5). The Warren Commission was basically handed a "lone nut" narrative that had been created by the FBI.

I wanted to brush away the cobwebs of the lone nut story and return to the authentic, lived experience of the people who witnessed the events of those two hours. In their statements, the witnesses remind us that events as they actually happened did not fit neatly into the Warren Commission's narrative. A haunting fact comes to us through the haze of history: It is unlikely that Oswald shot anyone that day.

I don't know who shot Kennedy, or who shot J.D. Tippit. But this is clear to me: The story constructed by the FBI and the Warren Commission falls apart under close scrutiny. Precisely how and why it falls apart will become evident in this timeline.

We can no longer accept the official story. It is simply a pop-culture myth, and nothing more.

As an English teacher, I am interested in the characters who were caught up in this drama while going about their daily lives. The details revealed by these witnesses achieve an accidental poetry to me; their stories have an innocence that is sometimes poignant, sometimes even humorous (Oswald's co-workers racing each other down to the first floor for lunch). The brief moments before the assassination seem idyllic in the horrific light of what followed.

I wanted to recover the humanity of the people involved in the assassination, and the heroism of the witnesses who merely told the truth about what they had seen and heard that day. The fragmentary nature of the witnesses' stories, when juxtaposed, achieve what I think is a fascinating, accidentally postmodern effect. We are reminded that truth is elusive, and it is a hard lesson to learn for those of us who crave certainty. And here I must apologize: there is little certainty to be found in this timeline.

Most of all, in doing this research, I wanted to decipher, as best I could, the enigma that was Lee Harvey Oswald. Because he was taken from us before he could tell his story, and before he could be given a fair trial, we must reconstruct from the fragments what his experience was on that day, as he left the Texas School Book Depository, embarked on his odyssey across Dallas, and was captured in the Texas Theater. I have tried to confront the question, *what was Oswald doing in those two hours*? We can only guess, but we can guess intelligently; and that is the point of this project.

What fascinates me is the fact that at 12:00, Oswald was a harmless warehouse worker on an ordinary day in Dallas. By 2:00 his fate had been sealed, and the country was forever changed. The angry crowd outside the Texas Theater reminded me of Meursault in Camus's *The Stranger*. The whole story of Oswald becomes a paranoid allegory for modern man.

Oswald's odyssey was America's odyssey, and every minute of it is immensely important, because every detail can help us solve the fundamental mystery of what he really did on that day.

It matters where Oswald was at 12:30 on November 22nd.

It matters what Oswald did immediately after the assassination, and how he behaved.

It matters if a false narrative was created after the assassination; and if it was, we must learn how it was constructed and who performed the cover-up.

My timeline attempts to answer these questions.

Andrew Culver

Sources are cited in-text; the Warren Report and its 26 volumes of testimonies and documents, as well as its many exhibits, are available on both maryferrell.org and The Assassination Archives and Research Center (aarc.org). WC denotes Warren Commission; CD denotes a Commission Document; and CE is a Commission Exhibit. The report of the House Select Committee on Assassinations (HSCA) has been of some use to me. These sources are all available at the above websites and they are easily searchable. Radio broadcasts are all available on YouTube. The Dallas Police radio transcripts are available at John McAdams's website (mcadams.posc.mu.edu) and in Commission Document 728. Since there are discrepancies, I have consulted both.

Oswald's Odyssey

11:55 – Lee Harvey Oswald is seen on the 5th or 6th floor of the Texas School Book Depository Building by his coworkers Bonnie Ray Williams, Danny Arce, and others, as they leave the 6th floor to get their lunches on the first floor. The employees are playing a game in which they take two separate elevators and race to the bottom floor. Oswald says, "Guys, how about an elevator?" or something to that effect, but fails to catch an elevator. This is the last time Oswald is seen before the assassination (WC testimonies). Oswald will later claim that he was eating his lunch in the presence of James Jarman and at least one other employee when the motorcade arrived, but this is unsubstantiated.

Williams gets his lunch and takes it back up to the 6th floor to eat shortly after 12:00.

Shortly before 12:00, Lee Bowers, Jr., stationed in the Union Terminal Tower in the railroad yard behind the fence on the grassy knoll, sees a car enter the parking lot. This is an extremely dirty 1959 Oldsmobile station wagon with an out of state license, driven by a middle-aged male (HSCA V, from FBI statement, Nov. 22).

12:15 – Bowers sees a second car enter the lot, this one a 1957 Ford Tutor with a Texas license. This man is talking into a radio transmitter and appears to be a police officer.

12:15 – According to statements made to the police and FBI on the 22nd and 23rd, Arthur Rowland, while standing at Houston and Main, sees a man with a rifle with a scope standing at the 6th floor window of the TSBD, at the southwest side of the building, which is closest to the Elm Street overpass (not Oswald's sniper's nest). The man is slender, with dark hair and a light collarless shirt which is open at the neck. He cannot identify the man as Oswald (HSCA V. 12).

12:15-12:20 –Bonnie Ray Williams is eating lunch alone on the 6th floor of the building, between the 3rd and 4th windows, facing Elm Street. At "approximately 12:20" he finishes his chicken lunch. He puts his Dr. Pepper and his lunch bag on the floor and leaves the 6th floor, taking the elevator to the 5th floor to join his friends Harold Norman and James Jarman. He does not see anyone else on the 6th floor at this time (WC testimony).

Williams has been working on the 6th floor since 8:00 AM with Charles Givens, Bill Shelley, Danny Arce, Billy Lovelady, and Harold Norman. He has seen Oswald once on the 6th floor shortly after 8:00, and once shortly before noon on the 5th or 6th floor, just before he went downstairs to get his lunch.

Jim Bishop *(The Day Kennedy Was Shot),* and other lone nut theorists, imagine Oswald waiting patiently on the 6th floor for 30 minutes before the motorcade, planning his shot. There is simply no evidence to place him there, however.

12:22- Lee Bowers sees a third car enter the lot, this one a 1961 or 62 Chevrolet Impala. The driver is about 30, with long dirty blonde hair, wearing a plaid shirt, and the car is very dirty. All three of the cars are gone after the assassination (HSCA, from FBI statement, Nov. 22).

12:25 (estimated) –James Jarman and Harold Norman, who are standing on the sidewalk in front of the TSBD waiting for the motorcade, decide to go up to the 5th floor for a better view of the President. They are joined by Bonnie Ray Williams (WC testimonies).

12:25 – This is the scheduled time for the motorcade to pass through Dealey Plaza, but it is running five minutes late. Any assassin who is aware of the motorcade schedule must be in place by this time.

12:29 – Immediately before the motorcade, Carolyn Walther, while standing on the east side of Houston Street, sees a man in the southeast corner of the TSBD, in the 4th or 5th floor window, with a rifle in his hands. He is wearing a light shirt and has light brown or blonde hair. Next to this man is another man wearing a brown suit coat. She is positive they are not on the 6th floor (HSCA V. 12, from FBI statement of Dec. 6).

12:30- The Presidential Motorcade begins the left turn onto Elm Street and slows down to 11 miles an hour. The motorcade is late; it was planned to pass through Dealey Plaza at 12:25, and 12:30 is the scheduled time for the motorcade to arrive at the Trade Mart. According to the Warren Report, "A Secret Service agent riding in the motorcade radioed to the Trade Mart that the President would arrive in 5 minutes."

In a strange deviation from common practice, there are no Secret Service agents riding on the back of the limousine. According to Secret Service researcher Vince Palamara (*Survivor's Guilt*), there is no evidence that President Kennedy (or anyone else) ordered the agents to keep off the back of the car, despite claims to the contrary by Secret Service agents after the assassination. Crucially, there are no agents running alongside the limousine, and motorcycle police have been placed behind or in front of the President's limousine – not to the side of it, where they could potentially protect the president. Additional anomalies of the Dallas motorcade: police have not been stationed on the roofs of buildings; the overpass is open to the public; the press vehicle, typically in front of the president's car has been placed far behind it and is now the 9th vehicle in the motorcade (leaving scant visual evidence of the assassination); no ambulance is present in the motorcade; the president's personal physician, Dr. Burkley, is in a bus far behind the president's limousine, where he would not be able to help the President in case of emergency; the slow speed of the motorcade (25 MPH was typical – 11 MPH was unheard of); a former defector to the Soviet Union (Oswald) is known to be working at a seven-story building on the route, with a clear view of the motorcade.

*Note (regarding the FBI's knowledge of Oswald): In July of 1963 the FBI learned of Oswald's contact with the FPCC, a pro-Castro group. According to Edward Jay Epstein (*Legend: The Secret World of Lee Harvey Oswald*), as early as October 10, the CIA informed the FBI that Oswald had visited the Cuban and Soviet Embassies in Mexico City on September 28, in an attempt to get a Visa to return to the USSR. According to the Church Committee (Book V), the FBI's New Orleans office knew on October 22 that Oswald had visited Vice Consul Kostikov at the Soviet Embassy in Mexico City, and that Kostikov worked for the wing of the KGB that dealt with assassinations and sabotage. On November 1 of 1963, FBI Agent James Hosty visited the residence of Ruth and Michael Paine in Irving, Texas (where Oswald and his family were staying) and was told by Ruth Paine that Oswald was working at the TSBD. About a week or ten days before the assassination, Oswald visited the FBI field office in Dallas and left a note for Hosty. According to the receptionists, it contained a threat that Oswald would blow up the FBI and the Police Department if they did not stop bothering his wife. FBI Special Agent in Charge of Dallas, Gordon Shanklin, instructed Hosty to destroy this note on November 24th after Oswald's death.*

According to an FBI memo of Dec. 6, the FBI gave the Secret Service no information on Lee Harvey Oswald prior to Nov. 22 (NARA Record # 180-10001-10416). After the assassination there was a bitter debate within the FBI about whether or not Oswald should have been on the Security Index. Hoover, believing Oswald should have been on the Index and should've been watched closely after his Mexico City trip, found gross negligence on the part of 16 FBI personnel, who received disciplinary action on December 16 (HSCA V). We must wonder, along with J. Edgar Hoover, why Oswald was allowed to be anywhere near the motorcade on that day. Of course, the "lone nut" explanation is that simple bureaucratic negligence was to blame for this oversight.

After the first shot, the driver of Kennedy's limousine, Secret Service agent William Greer, slows down the limousine, nearly bringing it to a complete stop. After the final shot, he accelerates and heads toward Parkland Hospital. Over sixty witnesses will later attest to Greer's slowdown. Between the first and final shots, Greer looks back at Kennedy twice, as can be seen on the Zapruder film. Palamara claims that according to eyewitnesses, and the Zapruder film, Greer is receiving communications through a radio microphone, which he is holding in his hand.

After the first shot hits Kennedy, Agent Emory Roberts, Commander of the Secret Service follow-up car (five feet behind JFK's limousine), orders other agents not to move. Clint Hill, who was not originally supposed to be on the Dallas trip but has come at the request of Mrs. Kennedy, jumps onto the back of the President's limo after the final shot (Palamara).

Secret Service agent Roy Kellerman (WC testimony) is riding in the front passenger seat of the President's limousine. As the motorcade proceeds down Elm Street he hears what sounds like a firecracker pop. He turns his head to the right, since the sound seems to have come from the right and the rear of him. He hears the President say "My God, I am hit." *As has been noted by other researchers, if this is true, the single bullet theory is impossible, since the first shot was supposed to have entered Kennedy's back, come out his throat (making it impossible to speak), and entered Governor Connally; if Kellerman is correct, the first bullet hit Kennedy in the back, and a separate bullet hit his throat.*

Kellerman turns around and sees that Kennedy has raised his hands up to his neck. Kellerman sees that Kennedy has been hit, and tells the driver, "Let's get out of here; we are hit." He radios Agent Lawson, in the front car, and says, "We are hit; get us to the hospital immediately." During the time he has been speaking, a "flurry of shells" comes into the car, and he turns around to see that Clint Hill is on the back of the car. Kellerman does not describe three separate shots, as the media will do later. He describes a flurry of instantaneous shots – *at least* two more shots after the initial shot. (It is fascinating to read Kellerman's WC testimony and to witness Gerald Ford and Arlen Specter try to coerce Kellerman into saying there were three distinct shots. While Kellerman refers to the first shot, and then a separate *flurry* of shots that sounded different from the first, Ford and Specter repeatedly refer to a first, second, and third shot.)

Kellerman tells the Commission, "President Kennedy had four wounds, two in the head and shoulder and neck. Governor Connally, from our reports, had three. There have got to be more than three shots." It is quite instructive to read Arlen Specter's condescending response to this, in which he tells Kellerman that this is just his "lay opinion." It is clear that as the architect of the single bullet theory, Specter had made up his mind long before all the evidence was available.

Clint Hill, riding in the follow-up car five feet behind the president (WC testimony), hears a shot from his rear and sees the President grab himself and lurch forward and to the left. He runs to the limousine, and as he reaches it, he hears a new gunshot, like someone firing a revolver into a hard object. This is clearly a different sound from the first. He struggles to gain a foothold on the car, and as he climbs onto the rear of the car, Mrs. Kennedy climbs onto the rear. She says, "My God, they have shot his head off." The second shot has removed a portion of the President's head and she seems to be climbing onto the back to retrieve it. He helps put Mrs. Kennedy back into the seat. He rides on the back of the car to the hospital. On the way to the hospital he sees that the right rear portion of the President's head is missing and his brain is exposed. Later he also notices the President's back wound – "about 6 inches below the neckline to the right-hand side of the spinal column."

(In Hill's WC testimony he firmly states that he heard two shots and no more, and that they were spaced about five seconds apart. He remembers looking at the triple underpass as the motorcade approached; there were about 5 or 6 people and a policeman on the underpass.)

Dallas PD officer Bobby Hargis, according to WC testimony, is riding his motorcycle at the rear left side of the President's limousine at 12:30. At the time of the first shot he sees the President bend over and Connally turn around. It appears that Connally has been hit first, but Hargis thinks he was mistaken about this. As Kennedy raises up, the shot that kills him hits him and Hargis is sprayed with "blood and brain, and kind of a bloody water. It wasn't really blood." Hargis can only recall two shots, but as he says, everything happened so fast, that there could have been 30 shots and he wouldn't have heard them. Hargis believes that the shots have come from the TSBD and the railroad overpass. He runs up the grassy knoll and looks at the overpass. Hargis looks at the TSBD and notices that no one near or in the building is looking toward the top of the building. Everyone in Dealey Plaza seems to be looking and running toward the overpass and the railroad yard. Hargis rides his motorcycle under the triple underpass and the Stemmons Freeway but does not see anyone fleeing the scene.

Officer Clyde Haygood, riding his motorcycle several cars behind the President, hears three shots (WC testimony): "The last two were closer than the first. In other words, it was the first, and then a pause, and then the other two were real close." David Belin, his interviewer, does not ask Haygood whether it is possible for one gun to fire both of the final shots, seeing as they were so closely spaced together. After the shooting Haygood speaks to James Tague, who has been struck on the cheek by a bullet fragment while standing by the triple underpass between Main and Commerce streets (in front of the President). A clear marking on the curb shows that a bullet, or a fragment, hit the street there. Since the Warren Commission has decided that only three shots were fired, James Tague must have been struck by one of them, and the wounds of Kennedy and Connally must have been caused by just two gunshots, thus necessitating the single bullet theory.

12:30 –Dallas Police Chief Jesse Curry, riding in the Presidential Motorcade, says into his radio, "Approaching triple underpass," and 19 seconds later he says "We are going to the hospital." This occurs at 12:30 (HSCA V. 2). This is according to the acoustical analysis of the Dallas police dictabelt recordings by Dr. James Barger for the HSCA.

From Officer Marion Baker's affidavit given on November 22, 1963 (CD 87): "Friday November 22, 1963 I was riding motorcycle escort for the President of the United States. At approximately 12:30 P.M. I was on Houston Street and the President's car had just made a left turn from Houston onto Elm Street. Just as I approached Elm and Houston I heard three shots. I realized these shots were rifle shots and I began to try to figure out where they came from. I decided the shots had come from the building on the northwest corner of Elm and Houston. This building is used by the Board of Education for book storage. I jumped off my motor and ran inside the building. As I entered the door I saw several people standing around. I asked these people where the stairs were. A man stepped forward and stated he was the building manager and that he would show me where the stairs were. I followed the man to the rear of the building and he said, 'Let's take the elevator.' The elevator was hung several floors up so we used the stairs instead. As we reached the third or fourth floor I saw a man walking away from the stairway. I called to the man and he turned around and came toward me. The manager said, 'I know that man, he works here.' I then turned the man loose and went up to the top floor. The man I saw was a white man approximately 30 years old, 5'9", 165 pounds, dark hair and wearing a light brown jacket."

From Commission Document 87, Secret Service report of December 8, 1963 (written by Special Agents Arthur Blake, William Carter and Elmer Moore): "[TSBD Superintendent Roy Truly stated that] the President's automobile passed his location at about 12:30 P.M., and a moment later three shots rang out. Almost immediately, Mr. Truly saw a motorcycle patrolman pushing through the crowd and heading for the entrance of the Depository Building. Mr. Truly ran inside the building with the patrolman, who asked 'Where is the stairway?' and Mr. Truly escorted him to the rear stairway. As they passed the shaft for the two freight elevators, Mr. Truly paused momentarily and, noting that neither of the elevators was available, he directed the way up the back stairway. As Mr. Truly started up the stairway from the second to the third floor, he noticed that the patrolman was not with him and, at the same time, he heard the patrolman say something. Mr. Truly returned to the second floor and saw the patrolman standing at the doorway leading to the lunchroom, with his pistol drawn and pointed at Oswald, who was then just inside the lunchroom just inside the doorway. The patrolman asked Mr. Truly if he worked in the building and Truly replied 'Yes.'"

Truly and the patrolman [Baker] continue up the stairs and take the elevator from the 5th to the 7th floors. They make a quick examination of the roof-top area, then come down the stairs, stopping briefly to make a quick search, and arrive at the first floor, where the employees of the TSBD are congregated. At this time Truly notices that Oswald is not present. He mentions to a police officer that Oswald is absent. Time for this event is not given in the Secret Service report.

From CD 5, FBI's Gemberling Report, "Interviews with Lee Harvey Oswald and Relatives," November 23, 1963: "Oswald stated that he went to lunch at approximately noon and he claimed that he ate his lunch on the first floor in the lunchroom; however he went to the second floor where the Coca-Cola machine was located and obtained a bottle of Coca-Cola for his lunch. Oswald claimed to be on the first floor when President Kennedy passed this building."

From Captain Fritz's "Interrogation of Lee Harvey Oswald," based on his handwritten notes (maryferrel.org), dictated on Jan. 10, 1964: (First interrogation, Nov. 22) "Mr Truly had told me that one of the police officers had stopped this man immediately after the shooting somewhere near the back stairway, so I asked Oswald where he was when the police officer stopped him. He said he was on the 2nd floor drinking a coca-cola [sic] when the officer came in. I asked him why he left the building, and he said there was so much excitement he didn't think there would be any more work that day, and that as his company wasn't particular about their hours, that they did not punch a clock, and that he thought it would be just as well that he left for the rest of the afternoon."

From "Interview with Lee Harvey Oswald by Postal Inspector, Dallas, Texas, 11/24/63": "When asked as to his whereabouts at the time of the shooting, he stated that when lunch time came, and he didn't say which floor he was on, he said one of the Negro employees invited him to eat lunch with him and he stated 'You go on down and send the elevator back up and I will join you in a few minutes.' Before he could finish whatever he was doing, he stated, the commotion surrounding the assassination took place and when he went downstairs, a policeman questioned him as to his identification and his boss stated that 'he is one of our employees' whereupon the policeman had him step aside momentarily. Following this, he simply walked out the front door of the building. I don't recall that anyone asked why he left or where or how he went. I just presumed that this had been covered in an earlier questioning" (Oswald 201 File Volume 20, *maryferrell.org*).

Note: The above account, as told by Oswald, places him near or at the entrance to the TSBD when Truly and Baker encounter him 90 seconds after the assassination (he went downstairs after his lunch, spoke to Baker and Truly, and simply walked out the front door). Notice how this is changed to the "3rd or 4th floor" in Baker's early account and finally the "2nd floor lunchroom" in later official accounts.

According to her affidavit of November 23, TSBD employee E.A. Reid watches the motorcade while standing on the front steps of the TSBD. After hearing the gunshots she walks back to her office on the second floor. She sees Oswald come through the back office door, which is located near the lunchroom and the rear stairway. He is wearing a white shirt and holding a Coke. She says "Oh! Someone has shot at the president. I hope they didn't hit him." Oswald mumbles something incoherent and walks out of the office.

From "Police Relate Story of Swift Capture," *NY Times* Nov. 23: "The first officer to reach the six-story building, Chief Curry said, found Oswald among other persons in a lunchroom. He said the building manager identified Oswald as an employee of the book-distribution concern that used the building. Oswald was not questioned then. When the main force of investigating officers reached the building Oswald had left. He became a suspect after the police had found on the sixth floor the rifle they believed was the assassination weapon. An elevator operator, the chief said, recalled having taken Oswald to the top floor before the motorcade passed by" (this is not corroborated anywhere else, and noon is the last time Oswald was seen before the assassination).

CE 2180 – Washington Post, Nov. 26: "A police officer, immediately after the assassination, ran in the building and saw this man in a corner and tried to arrest him; but the manager of the building said he was an employee and it was alright. Every other employee was located but this defendant of the company. A description and name of him went out by police to look for him."

Note- In CD 706, the FBI's collected statements of TSBD employees, there is no evidence of Truly locating every employee and noticing Oswald's absence. According to CD 706, many employees watching the motorcade were not allowed back in the building immediately after the shooting – they were finally let back in the building after 2:00, when the employees stuck inside were finally allowed to leave. There is no evidence of Truly making a "headcount" or checking up on the employees of the building, which consisted of various businesses. Many employees besides Oswald were also missing at the time of the search of the building. These people had left the building to go to lunch or watch the motorcade, and were not allowed back in after 12:30. The question arises: Why was Oswald singled out after Truly told Baker that he was "okay"? Regarding this point, see 1:25 below.

O.V. Campbell, Vice President and Secretary of the TSBD, in the statement from Nov. 26, 1963, by FBI

Special Agent Richard Harrison (CD 5): "Regarding events that occurred on November 22, 1963, Mr. Campbell advised he had viewed the Presidential Motorcade and subsequently heard the shots being fired from a point which he thought was near the railroad tracks located over the viaduct on Elm Street. He advised he had not heard anyone fire shots from their building; however, an individual wearing a construction-type hat was talking about seeing an individual fire from the window of the Texas School Book Depository building and he noted that a police officer had taken this individual's name.

"He further advised later in talking with Mrs. E.A. Reid, who is supervisor for the clerical staff for Texas School Book Depository, she had advised him she observed Lee Harvey Oswald in the second floor, at which time he had a Coca Cola in his hand and was presumed to have left by the front entrance.

"Mr. Campbell advised he had never met Mr. Oswald and knew nothing about him, in fact, could not recognize him inasmuch as the employees of the warehouse are handled by Mr. R.S. Truly, Director of Personnel."

According to *Life Magazine* (Feb. 21, 1964), Campbell hears someone say, "I saw a young man poke a rifle out that window right there and fire and draw back in."

According to WC (Warren Commission) testimony: TSBD employee Buell Wesley Frazier, standing on the front steps of the TSBD, watches the Presidential motorcade go by and hears several shots come from the direction of the railroad yards. After a few minutes he goes back into the building and eats his lunch in the basement. He tells the WC that the last time he had seen Oswald was between 10 and noon.

12:30 – According to her statement live on Dallas radio station KLRD at around 1:30, Mary Moorman, standing 15 feet from the President's limousine, hears two shots and sees the President grab his chest. Then the motorcade slows down. Then she hears three or four more shots, and the limo speeds off to the triple underpass. The police then run off in the direction of the gunshots, up the grassy knoll. She states that the shots were coming right at her. In the same interview, Jean Hill echoes this statement.

12:30: Howard Brennan is watching the motorcade from the south side of Elm Street, about 20 feet west of the southwest corner of Elm and Houston Streets (CD 5, in a report by FBI Special Agents Gaston Thompson and Robert Lish written on November 22). After hearing the gunshot or shots, he looks up to the window on the 6th floor near the southeast corner of the building. He observes a man with a heavy rifle in his hands. Only half of the rifle's length is protruding out of the window and Brennan cannot tell if it has a telescopic sight or not. The man fires another shot, taking deliberate aim at the President's limo, and then holds the rifle by the barrel as if it is resting on the floor. The man looks down at the street briefly and then walks away from the window. Brennan's distance to the window is approximately 90 yards and is unobstructed. Brennan sees a stack of boxes in the window, to the rear of the area in which the man is standing. Brennan describes the man as "early 30's, 5'10" tall and around 165 in weight," which, in a remarkable coincidence, corresponds exactly to the incorrect physical description of Oswald in his CIA 201 file dating back to 1959 (see notes for 12:45 below).

It is debatable whether Brennan could correctly identify the weight, age and height of someone 90 yards away, when standing on the ground and looking through a window on the 6th floor. There is no mention in this report that Brennan gave this description to the police immediately after the shooting. Brennan later identifies Oswald in a police lineup as the man most similar to the one he saw in the window, but he *cannot positively identify Oswald as the shooter*. Brennan's testimony seems to have become a smoking gun for lone nut theorists.

According to the affidavit of Dealey Plaza witness S.M. Holland, given in the Dallas Sheriff's Department on November 22, 1963: "I was standing on top of the triple underpass and the President's car was coming down Elm Street and when they get just about to the arcade I heard what I thought for the moment was a fire cracker and he slumped over and I looked over toward the arcade and trees and saw a puff of smoke come from the trees and I heard three more shots after the first shot but that was the only puff of smoke I saw. I immediately ran around to where I could see behind the arcade and did not see anyone running from there. But the puff of smoke I saw definitely came from behind the arcade through the trees. After the first shot the President slumped over and Mrs. Kennedy jumped up and tried to get over into the back seat to him and then the second shot rang out. After the first shot the secret service man raised up in the seat with a machine gun and then dropped back down in the seat. And they immediately sped off. Everything is spinning in my head and if I remember anything else later I will come back and tell Bill" (WC V. 20).

At the time of the shots, Lee Bowers, Jr., sees two men standing by the trees about 10 or 15 feet apart, directly in his line of vision between himself and the mouth of the overpass. These men are watching the motorcade. One of them is middle-aged, heavy-set, white shirt and dark trousers, and the other is mid-twenties, wearing a plaid shirt or jacket. After the shooting a policeman runs up the grassy knoll and there is some kind of commotion between the three. The younger man is hard for Bowers to see because he is obscured by trees (WC testimony, from HSCA V. 12).

TSBD employee Dolores Kounas is watching the motorcade 15 feet west of the southwest corner of Houston and Elm Streets. When the President is shot, she does not look toward the TSBD, as she thinks the shots have come "from the westerly direction in the vicinity of the viaduct." Billy Lovelady, who is standing on the front steps of the TSBD during the shooting, repeats this statement about shots coming from the viaduct. He recalls talking to Oswald on the 6th floor that morning, when Oswald asked him where a certain book was stored (CD 706, from statements in March, 1964).

Jean Hill, just a half hour after the shooting, is interviewed live on WBAP radio in Dallas, at the scene in Dealey Plaza. She says: "The shots came from the hill. It was just east of the underpass." The shots originated across the street from where she was standing, 10 or 15 feet away from the President when he was shot. When asked if she saw anyone on the hill after the shots, she says, "I thought I saw a man running."

According to WLW live radio coverage immediately following the assassination, reports of wounds indicate that the president was "shot in the right temple and the bullet went cleanly through the head."

Jack Dougherty, TSBD employee, is on the 5th floor, having just come down from the 6th floor when he hears gunshots. He goes down to the 1st floor where he speaks to Eddie Piper, who tells him the President has been shot (and mentions three gunshots). Dougherty goes up to the 6th floor, using the elevator, and sees no one there (From FBI statement on December 12, 1963, in Oswald's 201 File Volume 20). From same source, Eddie Piper states that he was on the first floor of the TSBD looking out the window at the motorcade when the shots ring out. He does not see Oswald at any time after the shots.

According to WC testimonies, TSBD employees James Jarman, Harold Norman, and Bonnie Ray Williams are on the 5th floor watching the motorcade as the President is shot (none of them mention Dougherty being on the 5th floor). Debris falls from the ceiling onto Williams's hair. Neither of the men hear anyone running upstairs, but Norman hears the bolt action of the rifle and the shells hitting the floor. About a minute after the final shot, they run down the stairs and exit the building, and do not see Oswald at any time. Once they arrive on the street, James Jarman sees Howard Brennan talking to a police officer. Jarman overhears Brennan telling the officer that he saw the barrel of a gun sticking out of the window on the 6th floor. There is no mention of Brennan's physical description of Oswald.

In a slightly different version of this story: After the shooting, Bonnie Ray Williams, who has been watching the motorcade from the 5th floor with Hank Norman and James Jarman, run to the west end of the building to get a better view. While they are there, a police officer comes up on the elevator and looks all around the 5th floor and leaves. Williams does not see or hear anyone come down the 5th floor on the stairs (CD 706, from a statement on March 19, 1964). It is unclear why this version involves the policeman, presumably Baker, encountering them, while their WC testimonies omit that.

NBC cameraman John Holfen is riding four cars behind the president's limo, turning onto Elm Street. He hears four shots. He sees the motorcycle cops run up the hill to the rail yards. He states that the police who searched the railroad yard have picked up a few suspects (WLW radio live coverage).

NBC correspondent Robert Pierpoint, riding in the motorcade, hears "a couple of explosions, maybe three." According to Pierpoint, the first shot hits the President in the Adam's apple, and Governor Connally turns around. In the process of turning around, Connally is hit by a second shot in the back (this makes the single bullet theory impossible). NBC reporters for KLRD remark on the amazing marksmanship of the sniper, firing at a moving target from the 5th or 6th floor of the building. They remark that it must have been a well-planned assassination, "not a spur of the moment affair." (From a live report on KLRD radio, around an hour and a half after the shooting.)

Note: Regarding the "well-planned assassination": The exact route for the motorcade (without maps) appeared in the Dallas Times Herald and the Morning News of November 19 (CD 3). A map of the route, including the *important turn down Elm Street, appeared in the* Dallas Times Herald's *final edition of November 21 (Palamara). This brings up the fact that Oswald, as he brought his rifle to work on the morning of the 22nd, had three days at the most to plan his assassination, and that assumes he was paying close attention to the newspapers' publications of the motorcade routes. (He also would not have had much time to create his sniper's nest and plan his shot in private, seeing that the motorcade was scheduled to arrive at 12:25 and he wasn't on the 6th floor at 12:20 when Bonnie Ray Williams was eating his lunch there.) The Secret Service report, in CD 3, claims that since the Trade Mart was announced as the final destination of the motorcade route on November 15, that the assassin could logically assume that the motorcade would use Elm Street, since that is the only way to enter the Stemmons Freeway. But, as researchers have noted before, there were many ways of getting to the Trade Mart from downtown. As Palamara says in* Survivor's Guilt, *"Prior to November 18, the motorcade route in Dallas was to have proceeded straight down Main Street." It is unclear even to this day who changed the route to include the slow left turn onto Elm Street, which violated Secret Service protocol.*

Even if Oswald knew that the motorcade was going through Dealey Plaza, his knowledge of the odd turn down Elm Street would be essential to the success of the assassination, considering that any other route would place Kennedy farther from the sniper's nest. None of Oswald's coworkers mentioned that he had any interest in the President's visit or the motorcade route (Williams mentioned seeing Oswald occasionally reading a newspaper and laughing to himself). FBI analysis of the map found in Oswald's room (CD 205) reveals that the X's placed on the map were in fact related to places where Oswald had applied for work, in addition to bus routes that he could take since he didn't drive a car. This map had no connection to the JFK motorcade route.

Additionally, in CD 345, the FBI's unofficial inventory of physical evidence, we find none of the three newspapers that would indicate that Oswald was studying the motorcade route. If he knew about it at all, it would have been through a coworker, but no one testified as to discussing the route with him. In fact, almost none of his coworkers had ever spoken with him. Bonnie Ray Williams told the Warren Commission that he hadn't heard any of his coworkers at the TSBD discussing the President's visit to Dallas (or the motorcade route) until the day of the assassination. In his testimony at the Garrison trial on February 13, 1969, Buell Frazier stated "We learned that morning that the President was due to come by about 12:00, so you don't get to see the President of the United States every day, so we all went outside to watch the parade."

Regarding the turn down Elm Street, employee James Jarman (Junior) testified that he spoke with Oswald on the 1st floor between 9:30 and 10:00 on the 22nd, and Oswald asked why people were gathering on the street corner in front of the building. Jarman told Oswald that the President was coming by. Oswald asked which way the President was coming, and Jarman told him he would probably come on Main, turn onto Houston, and then turn onto Elm. Oswald said "Oh," and walked away. So we have no evidence that Oswald knew about the motorcade route before 9:30 that morning. And there is no evidence of Oswald knowing the motorcade's *precise arrival time; Frazier said the employees thought the motorcade would arrive at noon.*

Jim Bishop claims that Oswald borrowed a copy of the Dallas Herald *from someone at work during lunch on the 21st where he saw the chart of the motorcade route. (The map was only published in the paper's evening edition, so this story might be a fiction.) Bishop claims that two hours after seeing the motorcade route at lunch, Oswald asked Buell Frazier for a ride to Irving that night, where he allegedly picked up the rifle that he brought to work the next day. Bishop's source for the newspaper story is unclear (possibly Frazier), and it appears to be unique to Bishop's book.*

The Dallas Morning News, *in their Nov. 22 article "Thousands Expected to Greet JFK," fails to mention the motorcade route (CD 678). Jim Lehrer's article on the Secret Service's preparations for the Dallas visit also neglects to mention the route. In fact, none of the 22 articles from local newspapers concerning JFK's Texas trip from the morning of November 22nd, featured in CD 678, mention the motorcade route. Buell Wesley Frazier, who gave Oswald a ride back to the Paine's residence in Irving on the 21st, and gave him a ride to the TSBD the morning of the assassination, did not discuss the President's visit with Oswald, and definitely did not see Oswald with any of the newspapers that would have provided information about the turn down Elm Street (WC testimony).*

Also, regarding the planning of the assassination, it is interesting to note that Oswald's passport application from June 24, 1963 (CE 781), filed in New Orleans, shows that he was planning to be in Cuba or Russia on November 22. His application specifically states that he is planning on leaving the country from October of 1963 to January of 1964. He had no intention at that time of being in America during JFK's trip to Dallas. He was still attempting to travel to Russia and/or Cuba at the beginning of October during his trip to Mexico.

According to the Warren Report, it was September 26 when Texas newspapers first reported that the President would visit Dallas, Fort Worth, San Antonio, and Houston on November 21-22. Even the Warren Report concludes that Oswald would only have had three days to plan the assassination, given that the motorcade route wasn't made public until the 19th, and that he did not get the job at the TSBD (which he started on October 15) with the intention of using it to assassinate the President. If Oswald acted alone, it seems all the more amazing that the assassination was so successful. As the Warren Report tells us, the administration had been planning the Texas trip for almost a year. Such a "well-planned," successful assassination ("not a spur of the moment affair") is more likely to be accomplished by someone with more advanced knowledge of the trip, and much more experience as a sniper, than Oswald had.

Also, Oswald's chances of success were statistically low. In a 2015 study, Benjamin Jones and Benjamin Olken collected data on assassinations of political leaders from 1875 to 2004. While 59% of assassination attempts were made by people ostensibly operating alone, only 25% of all assassination attempts were successful, and guns only killed the intended targets 31% of the time. Historically, assassins operating alone had a 29% chance of killing their target. For Oswald to succeed with these odds, no sniper experience, and only three days to plan, is indeed remarkable.

According the the FBI's Gemberling Report (CD 5), the distance from the sniper's nest to the first shot that hit Kennedy was 170 feet, and the distance to the head shot was 260 feet. This is well within the expectations for a military sniper, who may be expected to strike a target up to 900 meters or more. However, the qualifications for being such a sniper are daunting. The US Army Sniper Training Manual *provides criteria for a successful sniper. These include marksmanship, physical condition, vision, stable mental condition, intelligence (to operate all necessary equipment), emotional balance, and field craft, among others. Oswald, who was dyslexic, physically slight, untrained in marksmanship, and mentally unbalanced, had few of these qualities, and he had not been in the Marines for four years.*

The manual tells us correct preparation for the sniper to successfully hit his mark. These include choice of location, deciding the correct firing position from the many that are available (kneeling, standing, etc), placement of non-firing hand correctly under the butt of the rifle, correct placement of the butt in the shoulder, correct stance in order to provide bone support, consistent placement of the cheek with each shot, muscle relaxation, time to aim correctly, proper breathing techniques during the shot, locking the non-firing arm to absorb the rifle's recoil, correct head placement to avoid injury to the eye from the scope, judgment of distance and angle, sight alignment, usage of dominant eye for sighting, and calling the shot ("being able to tell where the round should impact the target").

A competent sniper would have to thoroughly understand muzzle velocity, line of sight, line of departure, trajectory, midrange trajectory, bullet drop, time of flight, retained velocity, gravity, drag, temperature, altitude/barometric pressure, humidity, wind, and efficiency of the bullet. Engaging a moving target requires leading (placing crosshairs ahead of the target's movement); analyzing speed of target, angle of movement, and range to target; wind effects; and tracking of the target. Needless to say, this is an incredibly complex task; military snipers work in teams for this reason.

If we are truly going to imagine Oswald successfully accomplishing this assassination, we must understand precisely what this would require. Accomplishing a successful strike on a distant moving target obviously requires enormous preparation and experience. It is quite easy to judge whether or not Oswald has all the requirements described above; his life is well documented, and even the Warren Report provides a biographical sketch. Norman Mailer's Oswald's Tale, *while perpetuating the lone nut myth, is a thorough examination of Oswald's life from 1959 to 1963. Unfortunately, everything Mailer and the Warren Commission say about him makes us less confident that he fits the sniper's qualifications above. Remember, Oswald would not have had much time to aim, given that the tree below the window on Elm Street obstructed the view of the President just before the first shot (CD 88). Interestingly, according to the sniper training manual, a moving target should always be shot from the front, as the target approaches the sniper, and snipers should position themselves very carefully around the target. When we consider that Oswald probably had about 5 minutes to prepare to shoot the president, and probably didn't know about the turn down Elm Street until 9:30 that morning, it becomes difficult to imagine him succeeding.*

12:31 - After the last shot, the boxes next to the window on the 6th floor are immediately moved.

The HSCA panel's analysis of the Dillard and Powell photographs, showing the 6th floor window, shows that the boxes in the window were moved between the time of the Dillard photo (taken a few seconds after the last shot) and the Powell photo (taken 30 seconds after the last shot). The FBI found that all the boxes by the window were movable by one man: two of them were fifty-five pounds while the rest were eight pounds (CD 1494). This does not tell us, however, how or why Oswald moved the boxes alone in less than 30 seconds.

Additionally, the HSCA's photographic analysis of the Phillip Willis no. 5 photograph identifies a person standing behind the wall on the grassy knoll at a time period that is simultaneous with the first shot (HSCA Vol. 6 ch. 5).

At the time of the shooting and immediately afterward, 40-year-old TSBD employee Jack Dougherty is on the 5th floor of the building, standing 10 feet from the elevator. He does not see Oswald and does not see any strangers in the building. He stays in the building until 1:30 (CD 706, from a statement on March 18, 1964).

12:31½ - William Manchester (*The Death of a President*) has Baker and Truly encountering Oswald in the 2nd floor lunchroom at this time, giving Oswald 90 seconds to descend four flights of stairs without being seen by Victoria Adams or Sandra Styles, who were descending the stairs from the 4th floor at that time. Baker vouches for Oswald, telling Truly he is an employee, and the two ascend the stairs.

Fritz's "Interrogation" of November 23, 10:35 AM: "In talking with [Oswald] further about his location at the time the president was killed, he said he ate lunch with some of the colored boys who worked with him. One of them was called 'Junior' and the other one was a little short man whose name he did not know. He said he had a cheese sandwich and some fruit and that was the only package he had brought with him to work and denied that he had brought the long package described by Mr. Frazier and his sister." Note: James Jarman, whose nickname was Junior, told the Warren Commission that he did have his lunch in the lounge on the first floor but did not see Oswald there.

CE 1987 (FBI Report Nov. 25, 1963)- Oswald stated that on November 22, 1963, he had eaten lunch in the lunch room in the Texas School Book Depository, alone, but recalled possibly two Negro employees walking through the room during this period. He stated possibly one of these employees was called 'Junior' and the other was a short individual whose name he could not recall but who he would be able to recognize. He stated that his lunch had consisted of a cheese sandwich and an apple which he had obtained at Mrs. Ruth Paine's residence in Irving, Texas, upon leaving for work that morning."

12:31 – Vincent Bugliosi (*Reclaiming History*) has Truly ascending the stairs to the third floor, while Baker reaches the top of the second floor stairs and scans the floor. Baker looks through the windows of the doors to the second floor, where he sees Oswald about twenty feet away, walking away from him toward the lunchroom. Baker enters the doors, points his gun at Oswald and says "Come here." Oswald calmly walks toward Baker, coming to within three feet. Truly, who has approached at this time, tells Baker that Oswald works in the building. Bugliosi does not mention a Coke or the Coke machine.

12:32 (estimated)- According to *Life Magazine*, Baker and Truly run into the building and find the elevators inoperable. They run up to the second floor. As Truly is walking up the stairs to the third floor, he notices that Baker is not with him. He runs back to the lunchroom to find Baker pointing his gun at Oswald, who is standing with his back to the Coke machine. Truly states that Oswald is an employee and the two continue up the stairs, leaving Oswald in the lunchroom.

12:32- Manchester has Baker searching the roof of the TSBD at this time.

12:32- Police Transcripts

Chief Curry – Go to the hospital. Parkland hospital. Have them stand by. Get men up to that overpass. See what happened up there....Move all men available to the railroad yards and determine what happened and hold everything secure until homicide and other investigators can get in there.

Sheriff J.E. Decker – Have my office move all available men out of my office into the railroad to try to determine what happened in there. Pull every one of my men in there and hold everything secure until Homicide and other investigators should get there.

Curry – Looks like the president has been...Have Parkland stand by.

Dispatcher – They have been notified.

Patrolman R.L. Gross – Dispatcher on channel 1 seems to have his mike stuck.

Dispatcher – Unknown motorcycle – up there on Stemmons with his mike stuck open on channel one. Could you tell someone up there to tell him to shut it off?

Sgt S.Q. Bellah – Do you still want me to hold this traffic on Stemmons until we find something?

Curry- Keep everything out of this emergency entrance.

According to WC testimony (V.3), after the final shot, Dallas Police Officer Eugene Boone runs west across Houston Street and cuts across the grass behind the cement works. Some of the bystanders believe the shots came from the railroad yard, so he and other officers search the rail yards and don't find anything. They encounter a "colored boy working on one of the pullmans" and talk to a man named Bowers who works in the train tower who "didn't hear any shots, and he hadn't seen anybody racing around out there in the yard."

Victoria Adams, an employee for Scott, Foresman, and Company, in room 401 of the TSBD, watches the motorcade from her office with fellow employees Elsie Dorman, Sandra Styles and Dorothy Garner. At 12:30 they witness the assassination and watch the President's limousine leave Dealey Plaza. She clearly mentions hearing three shots. After the third shot, she and Sandra Styles run down the stairs and leave the TSBD, running toward the railroad where they had observed other people running. They are told to return to the building, which they do. She leaves the TSBD around 2:00 or 2:30. Crucially, she does not see Oswald on the stairs after the shooting. She does not remember seeing him at all that day and saw no strangers in the building (CD 706, from a statement on March 23, 1964).

Sandra Styles leaves the TSBD with Victoria Adams immediately following the shooting, going down the back stairs. She and Adams are told by a policeman to go back into the building through the front door. They enter the TSBD and take the elevator to the 4th floor. Styles does not see Oswald at any time between leaving the office and returning to her office (CD 706).

12:32-12:34 – Georgia Hendrix, a TSBD employee for Allyn and Bacon, Inc., in room 301, watches the motorcade in Dealey Plaza. After the shooting she goes back into the building and returns to her office on the third floor at 12:34. As she goes up to the third floor immediately after the shooting, she does not see Oswald fleeing, or drinking a Coke, and has no memory of seeing him at all that day. Presumably Oswald would have been either running down the stairs, getting a Coke, or leaving the building at this time, but he has not been seen by Hendrix, Sandra Styles or Victoria Adams (CD 706, from statement on March 24, 1964).

12:33 – According to CE 1120 this is the official time Oswald leaves the front door of the TSBD. Importantly, as we see in CD 706, none of the TSBD employees standing on the front steps saw Oswald leave that day. None of the employees who were allowed to go back to their offices following the shooting saw him leave. Indeed, not a single TSBD employee witnessed Oswald walk down the stairs or exit the building. These were people who worked with Oswald and recognized him. Oswald should have been noticeable, presumably being in a hurry to leave the scene.

According to Inspector Kelley (CD 87), "After firing the shots Oswald walked from the window across the sixth floor area, hid the weapon, walked to the stairs, down the stairs to the lunch room on the second floor, spent approximately 30 seconds in the lunch room and continued down the stairs and out the front door. TIME 2:25 average walking, 2:52 with elevator waiting."

According to the *NY Times'* Nov. 22 article "Ambush Building Chosen With Care," TSBD president Jack Cason says the following: "[S]omeone could have hidden on that floor for several days without being discovered. Reserve stocks of books are more readily available in the basement and on the second and fourth floors. Only when additional copies are needed did employees of the building have occasion to go to the sixth floor. These circumstances indicated that the killer was well aware of the layout of the building and the uses of the various floors. No elevator goes to the sixth floor from the front entrances. The killer would have had to get off the elevator on the fourth floor, walk to the back of the building and take the stairs or one of two freight elevators to reach the sixth floor."

12:33 (estimated)- According to *Life*, Oswald exits the lunchroom holding a Coke. E.A. Reid tells him that the President was just shot, and he mumbles incoherently.

12:33- Manchester and Bishop have Oswald leaving the TSBD through the front entrance, giving NBC's Robert MacNeil directions to a pay phone.

12:33- Dallas Police Radio Channel One becomes unstuck, allowing police to communicate on both channels (Bishop).

(CE 1992) From statement to FBI, Nov 25: Deputy Sheriff Roger Craig is standing on Main Street, 20 feet east of Houston when he hears what he thinks is a gunshot. He walks west on Main toward Houston when he hears two more gunshots. He crosses Main Street and meets a Dallas police officer who confirms the sounds of gunshots. He walks down to the Santa Fe railroad tracks and sees a woman in a car with her engine running. He takes her to Lummy Lewis, from the Dallas Sheriff's Office, who takes her name and information. He talks to a man standing at the southwest corner of the TSBD who states that he saw a man holding a rifle in the 6th floor window of the TSBD fifteen minutes before the shooting, but assumed the man was a Secret Service agent. Craig brings this man to Lummy Lewis.

Then Craig walks to the south side of Elm Street in front of the TSBD to look for gun ricochet marks on the pavement when he hears a sharp whistling sound. He then notices a man running from the TSBD on the grass toward Elm Street. A station wagon, which Craig believes was a Nash Rambler, is driving west down Elm Street and stops at the curb. The running man gets inside the car and the two leave, traveling west on Elm. Although Craig previously believed that the driver had been a Negro, he now believes the driver was white. He describes the running man as a white male, 5'9", 140 pounds, slender build, sandy hair, brown shirt and blue trousers. Later that afternoon Craig views Oswald at the police station and states that Oswald was the running man. There is no doubt in his mind of this fact.

Richard Randolph Carr, a bystander in Dealey Plaza, walks toward the triple underpass after the shots. He sees a man coming down Houston Street whom he had seen earlier in the fifth floor window of the TSBD. This man is wearing a felt hat, heavy rimmed glasses, a tie and a tan sportcoat. The man turns and walks down Commerce Street. He looks over his shoulder frequently as though being followed. Carr also notices a Rambler station wagon heading north on the wrong side of the street next to the TSBD facing the railroad tracks. Three men emerge from behind the depository and enter the station wagon. One of them is "dark-complected," and the car drives north on Houston Street. This is based on an FBI interview of January 1964 and Carr's testimony in the Clay Shaw trial in 1969 (HSCA V. 12).

Bystander James Worrell sees a man he believes to be Oswald leave through the back entrance of the TSBD, running on Houston from Elm to Pacific. This is based on a Dallas Police Department affidavit of November 23. (HSCA V. 12)

After the President's Limousine leaves Dealey Plaza Jean Hill sees a man running along the grassy knoll toward the monument (according to Dallas PD affidavit of November 22). In an FBI statement of March 13, 1964, she describes "a white man in a brown raincoat and a hat running west away from the depository in the direction of the railroad tracks." In the sheriff's office on Nov. 22, when she says there were 4 or 6 shots, *several men she describes as either FBI or Secret Service tell her it was actually three shots*. Hill tells the Warren Commission that the man she saw running away from the depository resembled Jack Ruby (HSCA V. 12).

Note- The refrain of "three shots" started so quickly on the day of the assassination and was so widespread that it is hard to pinpoint its origin – especially when many witnesses heard anywhere from two to six gunshots that day. But here, in Jean Hill's near-heroic testimony, we see one source of the "three shot" idea. One must wonder why witnesses' honest recollections were being "corrected," on the day of the assassination.

According to CE 2060, the Secret Service's November 29 report on the third interview with Oswald, "[Oswald] said that when he was standing out in front of the textbook building and about to leave it, a young crew-cut man rushed up to him and said he was from the Secret Service, showed a book of identification, and asked him where the phone was. Oswald said he pointed toward a payphone in the building and that he saw the man actually go to the payphone before he left."

NBC correspondent Robert MacNeil, from a statement of Nov. 30, in Oswald's 201 File (Volume 20): "It was the Texas School Book Depository. I believe I entered the front door about four minutes after the shooting. I went immediately into the clear space on the ground floor and asked where there was a phone. There were, as I recall, three men there, all I think in shirt sleeves. What, on recollection, strikes me as possibly significant is that all three seemed to be exceedingly calm and relaxed, compared to the pandemonium which existed right outside their front door. I did not pay attention to this at the time. I asked the first man I saw – a man who was telephoning from a phone by pillar in the middle of the room – where I could call from. He directed me to a man nearer the door, who pointed to an office...I made my call and left. I was in too much of a hurry to remember what the three men there looked like. But their manner was very relaxed. My New York news desk has since placed the time of my call at 12:36 Dallas time." Note that MacNeil's statement by no means implicates Oswald as the individual who gave him the directions to the phone.

12:34- UPI (United Press International) announces three shots fired at the motorcade (Manchester).

12:32-35 – Police arrest hobos Gus Abrams, John Gedney, and Harold Doyle in the railyard. From "Arrest Report on Investigative Prisoner (texashistory.unt.edu): "These men were taken off a train box car in the rail yards right after President Kennedy was shot. These men are passing through town. They have no jobs or any means of making a living."

12:34 – According to CD 677 (Secret Service Chief James Rowley's memo to Warren Commission General Counsel David Belin), the motorcade reaches Parkland Hospital at this time. According to this memo, the motorcade consists of the following:

1. Lead car, with Dallas Chief of Police, Sheriff Decker, SAIC Forest Sorrels, SA Winston Lawson
2. President's car, driven by William Greer, with ASAIC Roy Kellerman, President Kennedy, the First Lady, Governor Connally, and Mrs. Connally
3. The President's followup car, driven by SA Samuel Kinney, occupied by ASAIC Emory Roberts, SA Clinton Hill, SA William McIntyre, SA John Ready, SA Paul Landis, SA Glen Bennett, SA

George Hickey, and Mr. Dave Powers and Mr. Kenneth O'Donnell

4. Vice President's car, driven by Hurchel Jacks of Texas Department of Public Safety, occupied by ASAIC Rufus Youngblood, Vice President Johnson, Mrs. Johnson, and Senator Ralph Yarborough

5. Vice President's followup car, driven by Joe Henry Rich of the Texas Department of Public Safety, occupied by ATSAIC Thomas Johns, SA Jerry Kivett, SA Warren Taylor, and Mr. Cliff Carter of the Vice President's staff

12:35 -12:40- Police Transcripts

Patrolman C.A. Haygood- I just talked to a guy up here who was standing close to it and he could tell it came from the Texas School Book Depository building...with that Hertz renting sign...

Dispatcher- 10-4. Get his name, address, telephone number there – all the information you can from him.

Sgt. D.V. Harkness- I have a witness who says it came from the 5th floor of the Texas Book Depository Store.

Patrolman Hill – Get some men up here to cover this school book depository building. It's believed the shot came from, as you see it on Elm Street, looking toward the building, it would be upper right hand corner, second window from the end.

Hill- I have one guy who was possibly hit by a ricochet from a bullet off the concrete and another one who saw the president slump.

Brewer- We have a man here who says he saw him pull the weapon back through the window from the southeast corner of that depository building.

Dispatcher – Alright, do you have the building covered off?

Brewer- No, about ¾ of a block away from there.

Assistant Chief of Police Charles Batchelor – Where did this happen – at Field and Main?

Dispatcher- At Stemmons and the Triple Underpass, 12:40 P.M. 2 (Batchelor), there's a possibility that 6 or 7 more people may have been shot.

Patrolman William Price – I believe the President's head was practically blown off.

According to Captain Fritz, "While we were still searching the building, Mr. Roy S. Truly…reported that one of his men were missing, a Lee Harvey Oswald, whose address was 2515 W. 5th Street, Irving, Texas. We found that this man had been stopped by Officer M.L. Baker while coming down the stairs. Mr. Baker says that he stopped this man on the third or fourth floor on the stairway, but as Mr. Truly identified him as one of the employees, he was released. After seeing that this man was apparently running, two of the detectives and myself left the building and came to the office for an identification check and other information, and soon found that he was the same man who had shot Officer Tippit" ("Note from J.W. Fritz to Jesse Curry of 23 December 1963"). *Note: This account has Oswald running during the Baker-Truly encounter. This also repeats Baker's odd claim that Oswald was on the third or fourth floor.*

(CE 2146) WFAA TV Reel, "Interview with Police Chief Jesse Curry," November 23, 1963:

Q – What time is established – how Oswald got to the other side of town – is there anything that can be come up about – did he get over by a bus, by a car, did he have to walk?

Curry- I don't know. We have understood that he was picked up by a Negro in a car.

Q- That is not confirmed?

Curry – No, it is not confirmed, as far as I know.

Q- Are you looking for the Negro?

Curry – We would like to know about him if this is so; we would certainly like to find him.

Q- Chief Curry, would you detail for us what led you to Oswald?

Curry – Not exactly, except in the building, we, when we went to the building why he was observed in the building at the time; but the manager told us that he worked there and they passed him on the way up then because the manager said he is an employee.

Q- Is that before the shooting or after?

Curry- After...

Q- Did you say, Chief, that a policeman had seen him in the building?

Curry- Yes.

Q- After the shot was fired?

Curry – Yes.

Q- Why didn't he arrest him then?

Curry – Because the manager of the place told us that he was an employee. Said, "He's alright, he's an employee."

Q- Did he look suspicious to the policeman at this point?

Curry- I imagine the policeman was checking everyone he saw as he went into the building.

Q- Chief, after this happened, what was done in terms of getting the trail back to Oswald?

Curry – The next thing we know is when he turned up as a suspect in the murder of the police officer – and then the connection we made between the two.

12:33-12:36: Oswald walks to the bus stop.

Vida Lee Whatley, a TSBD worker, is shopping on Elm Street when the President is shot. She is walking on Elm between the Moses and Kress stores when a stranger tells her that the President has been shot. She does not see Oswald, on what is presumably his escape route to the bus stop (CD 706, from a statement on March 3, 1964).

CE 1987 (FBI Report dated November 25, 1963)- "The distance from the front door of 411 Elm Street (the Texas School Book Depository Building) to the bus stop at Murphy and Elm streets in Dallas was walked three times by SA Lee, and the average time was 6 ½ minutes. This is a distance of approximately 7 blocks."

From Kelley's timeline (CD 87): "Front door to Murphy and Elm Street where he boarded bus, via Main Street 7 blocks. TIME 4:30 minutes."

The two reports above give quite different time frames for Oswald's journey from the TSBD to the bus stop. If he left at 12:33, Kelley's timeline places him at the bus at 12:37, which is consistent with McWatter's testimony below, but the timeline from CE 1987 has Oswald getting on the bus around 12:40, when he should've been on the bus for several minutes already according to McWatters's schedule. Obviously this has importance because it determines when Oswald left the TSBD (and where he was when Kennedy was shot), assuming we believe that he did indeed get on the bus that day. It seems increasingly likely that, assuming he got on McWatter's bus, he left the TSBD immediately after the assassination at 12:30. This is the only way he would have time to walk the 7 blocks to the bus. See below, 12:40.

12:35 – *Life* has Oswald leaving through the front door of the TSBD at this time.

12:35-12:40 – From CD 1134: A 31-year-old man is arrested in the railroad warehouses near the TSBD. The man is armed at the time of arrest. (*Dallas Times Herald* Dec. 8, quoted in Joesten)

Unknown time - A man is arrested by Officer W.E.B. Barker on the third floor of the TSBD after being identified by employees. He is wearing horn-rimmed glasses, a checked jacket, and a raincoat. He is taken to Sheriff Decker's office across the street (*Dallas Times Herald* Nov. 22, qtd. in Joesten)

12:36 – ABC announces the shooting, breaking into pre-scheduled programming (Manchester).

12:36 – JFK reaches Parkland Hospital (Manchester).

12:36– Cecil J. McWatters, bus driver for the Dallas Transit Company, leaves the corner of Elm and St. Paul streets at 12:36, traveling down Elm Street in the direction of the TSBD. He has been ahead of his schedule so he has waited one minute before leaving the stop. He has stops at Ervay, Akard, and Field Streets. Traffic slows down and the bus comes to a stop at the corner of Elm and Field streets, where Oswald knocks on the door of the bus. McWatters lets him on and Oswald pays the 23 cent fare. Oswald is wearing "work clothes, just some type of little old jacket." He sits alone in the second cross seat. The bus travels two blocks and comes to a stop in heavy traffic. Before Oswald gets off, a man gets out of a car stuck in traffic ahead of the bus and enters the bus to inform McWatters that the President has been shot – this occurs between Poydras and Lamar. Three or four minutes have passed while waiting at this intersection. Oswald asks for a transfer and gets off the bus here. McWatters does not pay any particular attention to Oswald and does not remember anything notable about him. (WC Volume 2).

It should be noted that Cecil McWatters's bus is heading straight toward the corner of Houston and Elm streets, where it would turn left at Houston, pass the TSBD on its right (and the Sheriff's Department on its left), and travel south down Houston. It is strange to imagine Oswald taking a bus straight past the scene of the crime, which by now would be full of police looking for him. He would be heading into a place where the bus was likely to be pulled over and all its occupants searched by police (as it was, according to Milton Jones's FBI testimony). Oswald would have known the bus route, having taken it every day to and from work. Also, the Marsalis bus was a completely logical bus for him to take - going south down Marsalis it would have stopped, probably at 5th street, a 10 minute walk or short bus ride from his house at 1026 North Beckley.

Dallas City Attorney Henry Wade tells the *NY Times* on Nov. 24 that Oswald "told the bus driver that the president had been shot, and laughed" ("Evidence Offered," Nov. 24).

12:32-12:36- According to CE 1985, FBI report of Nov. 24, Mary Bledsoe, Oswald's former landlord at 621 N. Marsalis (who had evicted him), gets on McWatters's bus at St. Paul and Elm approximately ten minutes after she watches the motorcade pass by St. Paul and Main Street (12:22). Shortly after this, Oswald gets on the bus at Murphy Street. She states that Oswald got on, paid his fare, and went to the back of the bus, appearing "somewhat nervous." She remarks that he was wearing dirty clothes, which she considers strange considering that he always kept a clean appearance when rented a room from her. The driver tells the passengers that the President has been shot. Almost immediately Oswald gets off the bus, two blocks further down Elm Street than when he had gotten on. Oswald leaves through the front door of the bus, although the side door is closer. Bledsoe's testimony, while implicating Oswald as "somewhat nervous," suggests a far too early boarding time for Oswald, considering what he has had to do in this brief period of time (see below).

J. Edgar Hoover, in his conversation with Lyndon Johnson on 11/29 (maryferrell.org): "On that floor, we found the three empty shells that had been fired and one shell that had not been fired...in other words, there were four shells apparently and he had fired three, but didn't fire the fourth one. He then threw the gun aside and came down…at the entrance of the building…he was stopped by police officers and some manager in the building told the police officers, 'well, he's alright…he works there…you needn't hold him.' They let him go. That is how he got out. And then he got on a bus, bus driver has identified him and [he] went out to his home…and got hold of a jacket…that he wanted for some purpose…and came back downtown…walking downtown…and the police officer who was killed…stopped him…not knowing who he was and not knowing whether he was THE man…but just on suspicion…and he fired of course and killed the police officer…Then he walked…"

LBJ- You can prove that?

Hoover- Oh yes, oh yes, we can prove that.

12:37- Joesten places Oswald on Pacific Street, behind the TSBD, at this time, giving time for Oswald to drink his Coke, learn of the shooting (and that there would be no more work that day), talk to Truly and Baker, and to leave the building through the growing crowd of people. He attests that Oswald could not have been running, seeing as he would have been arrested as a suspect (as others were that day).
According to the Warren Report itself, McWatters's bus route was heading back in the direction of the TSBD on its way to Oak Cliff. Since Oswald took the bus every day, he clearly knew this.

12:38 – According to his WC testimony, Dallas Police Officer E.D. Brewer, investigating the scene of the crime, radios, "A witness says he saw 'em pull the weapon from the window of the second floor of the southeast corner of the depository building." Brewer is reading his statement from the transcripts provided to him in the WC interview. This statement is not on the transcripts provided to the WC in CD 728.

12:39 – Bugliosi has Oswald entering the bus.

12:39 – UPI reports that Kennedy is seriously wounded by an assassin's bullet (Bishop).

12:40 - Jack Ruby is seen at the *Dallas Morning News* offices, where he hears that the President has been shot (HSCA V. 9).

12:40 – *Life* and Manchester have Oswald entering the bus.

12:40 – Oswald most likely gets off the bus at this time. According to CE 378, Cecil McWatters's bus schedule, this is the time for the bus's arrival at Lamar, when the bus comes to a stop in heavy traffic, and a man gets on the bus to tell everyone that the President had just been shot. Oswald gets off the bus immediately after this. Recall that McWatters was on schedule up until the slowdown at Lamar. This means Oswald has already been on the bus sitting in traffic for several minutes. This creates a scenario in which Oswald leaves the TSBD at 12:33 (or 12:35 according to *Life*) and approaches the bus, 7 blocks away, sometime between 12:36 and 12:39, and gets on calmly, showing no signs of nervousness (according to McWatters and Jones), and *pays the correct fare*. In this scenario, in 6-9 minutes he has: shot and killed the president, moved the boxes in front of the window, stored his rifle in between two boxes on the opposite side of the building (see 1:23 below), run down six flights of stairs, gotten a Coke on the 2nd floor, calmly stood drinking it while Baker and

Truly run past him, left the TSBD through a panicking crowd of people, given directions to a payphone to someone he believed was a Secret Service agent, and traveled seven blocks on foot to calmly get on a bus that was heading back toward the scene of his crime.

Later that day, at 6:30, McWatters is unable to positively identify Oswald in a police lineup but says he looks similar to the man who knocked on the door of the bus. He describes Oswald as 135-140 pounds, around 5'7" or 5'8" and tells the Warren Commission that he had mistaken Oswald for a 17-year-old boy named Milton Jones who was also on the bus that day. McWatters refers to Oswald as the shortest man in the lineup and recognizes Oswald's transfer given to him by police as his own (given by him).

Google Maps gives the walking time from the TSBD to Elm and Field, where Oswald boarded the bus (according to McWatters), as 8 minutes. This has Oswald boarding the bus at 12:41 at the earliest, assuming he left the TSBD at the Warren Commission's given time of 12:33, which in itself is hard to believe. All of this forces one to accept that Oswald most likely left the TSBD almost immediately after Kennedy was shot, at 12:30. This, of course, places him on the first floor or on the steps of the front entrance of the TSBD, where Sean Murphy argues he was standing during the assassination (see Stan Dane's *Prayer Man: The Exoneration of Lee Harvey Oswald*). If, however, Oswald ran out of the TSBD and entered a Nash Rambler, as Roger Craig swore he did, the difficult timing of the bus entry is not an issue. It is by no means certain that Oswald did get on the bus.

12:40- Dallas Patrol Officer M.N. McDonald, on his way to Dealey Plaza, hears the description of the suspect: White male, approximately 27, 29 years old, and he had a white shirt on, weighed about 160 pounds" (WC 3). According to police dictabelt transcripts this couldn't have happened until 12:45. This description presumably comes from Howard Brennan, since he claims to have seen the shooter, but there is no evidence among the police transcripts that the 12:45 description came from him.

From Kelley's timeline (CD 87): "Bus ride to Elm and Poydras, 2 blocks. TIME 4:00 minutes average."

Captain Fritz's "Interrogation of Lee Harvey Oswald": (From interview with Oswald, Nov. 23, 10:35 AM) "During this interview I asked Oswald about leaving the building, and he told me he left by bus and rode to a stop near home and walked on to his house. At the time of Oswald's arrest he had a bus transfer in his pocket. He admitted this was given to him by the bus driver when he rode the bus after leaving the building."

From CE 2641 (FBI Letter, April 3, 1964): "On March 30, 1964, Roy Milton Jones, 512 East Brownlee Street, Dallas, Texas, advised he is an 11th grade student attending half-day sessions at the N.H. Crozier Technical High School, Live Oak and Bryan Streets, and is employed part time as a clerk at Buddies Supermarket, Tenth and Jefferson Streets, Dallas, Texas. Jones stated that he uses the name Milton Jones and is better known by this name at school and at work...

"Jones advised that before the bus was stopped the driver made his last passenger pickup approximately six blocks before Houston Street, that one was a blonde-haired woman and the other was a dark-haired man. He said that the man sat in the seat directly behind him and the woman occupied a seat further to the rear of the bus. Jones advised that when the bus was stopped by traffic, and prior to the appearance of the police officers, the woman left the bus by the rear door and the man who was sitting behind him left the bus by the front door while it was held up in the middle of the block. Jones stated he did not observe this man closely since he sat behind him in the bus, but, on the following Monday when he took the same bus going home from school from the same driver, the driver told him he thought the man might have been Lee Harvey Oswald...

"With regard to this man who sat behind him, Jones stated he did not notice anything unusual about the man when he boarded the bus or when he left it. He said the man was not carrying any packages and he certainly did not see a gun in his possession at any time. He said the man did not appear nervous or excited and seemed to him to be an ordinary passenger. He described this man as follows:

Race: White

Sex: Male

Age: 30-35

Height: 5'11"

Weight: 150

Build: Medium

Remarks: Wore no glasses and no hat

Hair: Dark brown, receding at temples

Dress: Light blue jacket and gray khaki trousers."

Note: Based on eyewitness testimony, it is still uncertain that Oswald did get on McWatters's bus. However, Oswald's possession of McWatters's transfer makes it more likely. What is remarkable is that Jones and McWatters did not notice anything odd about Oswald at the time. He clearly was not behaving suspiciously or nervously, less than 10 minutes after the assassination. Lone nut theorists have Oswald walking down 10th Street like a maniac at 1:15, 45 minutes after the assassination, behaving so strangely that he arouses the suspicions of J.D. Tippit. Similarly, we are told that Oswald was behaving like a maniac an hour after the assassination outside Johnny Brewer's shoe store, when he was quite calm between 12:31 and 12:45 (See William Whaley's testimony at 12:45). Of course, it is tempting to imagine Oswald realizing that he has been set up in some way; one can picture Oswald becoming more nervous and perhaps paranoid once he suspects he will be framed or involved with the assassination. This scenario would not be incompatible with Oswald's complex relationship with the CIA as detailed in John Newman's Oswald and the CIA.

12:43 – Bugliosi has Oswald exiting the bus at this time.

12:43-12:44 – Police Transcripts

Captain C.E. Talbert – Are you having them contain that block or 2 block area?

Dispatcher – Yes, we are trying to seal off that building until it can be searched.

Inspector J.H. Sawyer (9)– The weapon looked like a 30-30 rifle or some type of Winchester.

Dispatcher- 9, it was a rifle?

Sawyer- A rifle, yes.

Dispatcher – Any clothing description?

Sawyer- About 30, 5'10", 165 pounds.

Note: 12:44 is the earliest time this physical description appears on police transcripts, and we are not told through the transcripts who provided it. As we know, Oswald was in reality 24, and a shorter and lighter man (he gave his own height and weight as 5'9" and 150 pounds on his TSBD employment application on October 15, 1963). The erroneous 165-5'10" description of Oswald would not be notable if it weren't present in multiple government files dating as early as 1959 (when Oswald attempted to defect to the USSR), including FBI Agent Fain's report of 1961 (in which the description apparently comes from Oswald's mother) and in the CIA's 201 file on Oswald. Notable in the 201 file is a cable of October 10, 1963, regarding Oswald's mysterious trip to Mexico City, which describes him as "probably identical to Lee Henry Oswald" and lists his physical characteristics as "Five feet ten inches, one hundred sixty-five pounds, light brown wavy hair, blue eyes." See Peter Dale Scott's Dallas '63 *for more on the CIA's dissemination of false data on Oswald from 1959-1963. Ostensibly the description of the suspect given by Sawyer above is the reason that J.D. Tippit stopped Oswald on 10th street, even though Oswald was younger and smaller than that, and was several miles away from the crime scene. We must question the likelihood of Howard Brennan (or any other bystander) describing Oswald with the same incorrect weight-height combination the CIA had used for four years in confidential documents. As WC counsel Wesley Liebeler pointed out in his memorandum of September 6, 1964, there was simply no evidence that the Oswald description of 12:44 came from Brennan, and the Warren Report never explicitly claims that it did (HSCA Exchibit 36). What is also notable about the description above is the absence of clothing description. Notice that every single witness to Tippit's killer provides clothing descriptions to police at the scene. In the transcripts, officers ask the dispatcher multiple times if there any clothing descriptions of the Dealey Plaza suspect. This shows that it was normal and expected for witnesses to provide this information.*

12:44 – According to CE 1120, "Off bus, between Poydras St. and Lerner St." *Lerner must be a mistake for Lamar.*

From Kelley's Timeline (CD 87): "Elm and Poydras (walking) to cab stand, 4 blocks. TIME 3:00 minutes.)

CE 1987 – "The distance from the bus stop at Poydras and Elm streets to the cab stand at the northwest corner of Lamar and Jackson streets, four city blocks, was walked by SA Lee in three minutes."

Manchester has Oswald exiting the bus at 12:44.

12:45 – Bugliosi has Oswald getting in Whaley's cab at this time.

12:45– Dispatcher (Sergeant G.D. Henslee): "Attention all squads. Attention all squads. At Elm and Houston reported to be an unknown white male, approximately 30, slender build, height 5 feet 10 inches, weight 165 pounds, reported to be armed with what is believed to be a .30 caliber rifle. Attention, all squads, the suspect is believed to be a white male, 30, five feet ten inches, slender build, 165 pounds, armed with what is thought to be a 30-30 rifle. No further description or information at this time" (CD 1420).

Police Transcripts

233 –(Forston) – He is thought to be in this Texas School Book Depository here on Northwest corner Elm and Houston.

12:45 - Joesten believes Oswald could not have gotten on the bus until this time.

12:45- The dispatcher orders Patrolman R.C. Nelson and J.D. Tippit into Oak Cliff area. Tippit says he is at Kiest and Bonnieview. This is his last communication until 12:54. Silvia Meagher questions the reasoning for the orders to move into Oak Cliff, which "make no sense," and observes that no similar orders in the chaotic fifteen minutes following the assassination (for officers to move into areas other than downtown) were given to anyone besides Nelson and Tippit (qtd. in Joseph McBride, *Into the Nightmare*). See CD 1108 for confirmation of this. This FBI memorandum reports on the whereabouts and assignments of all police officers during and after the assassination. The vast majority of officers are assigned to the TSBD and immediate vicinity after 12:30. Those who are not at the TSBD are assigned to, or already at, Love Field or Parkland Hospital. A very few officers remain in their usual districts to set up road blocks. Tippit's assignment was unique in that he was told to leave his district and go to an area other than Dealey Plaza, Parkland Hospital, or Love Field. It is notable that Oak Cliff was where Oswald lived, and that this was before Oswald was a suspect – and that Tippit was the only officer other than Nelson who was sent there.

According to McBride, Tippit is *not* at Kiest and Bonnieview, where he claims to be. He is in fact at the Gloco gas station at 1502 North Zang Boulevard, watching the Houston Street viaduct and waiting for someone to cross it. This is according to five witnesses. Bishop has Tippit parking at the viaduct at Eight Street and Corinth Street, "sealing off one of the seven ways of getting out of downtown Dallas to the south." According to Bishop, after this, Tippit turns west into Oak Cliff and patrols the neighborhood. Bishop does not think it strange that Tippit is on this errand so far away from all locations relevant to the crime.

McBride states that Tippit's father (interviewed by McBride) claimed that Tippit's wife Marie had been told later about Tippit's duties after 12:30 by another police officer on duty that day. The elder Tippit claimed that his son and Officer Nelson had been sent to Oak Cliff for the express purpose of intercepting Oswald, who was supposed to be heading in that direction. Strangely, Officer Nelson did *not* move into Oak Cliff and instead went to Dealey Plaza, where he was at 12:51. Bugliosi does not question the purpose of dispatcher Murray Jackson ordering Nelson and Tippit into Oak Cliff, and does not question Nelson's disobedience, stating that Jackson "Decides to let him go."

12:45 (estimated)- *Life* has Oswald "running" two blocks to Whaley's taxi at this time.

12:48- Oswald enters William Whaley's taxi (CE 1120).

According to Manchester, Whaley thinks Oswald is a "wino two days off the bottle."

Unknown Time (WC V.2) – In WC testimony, William Whaley says he is parked at the Greyhound stand at Jackson and Lamar when he sees Oswald walking south down Lamar from Commerce. He doesn't pay much attention to Oswald's clothes, but it all comes back to him when he finds out who Oswald is later. Whaley describes Oswald's clothes as not khaki pants but khaki material, "like a blue uniform made in khaki... brown shirt with a little silverlike stripe on it...some kind of jacket, I didn't notice very close but I think it was a work jacket that almost matched the pants...his shirt was open three buttons down here. He had on a t-shirt. You know, the shirt was open three buttons down here."

Oswald says, "May I have the cab?" Whaley says, "You sure can. Get in." Oswald gets in the front seat. An old lady sticks her head in the cab and asks if Whaley can call her a cab. Oswald says, "I will let you have this one." She says, "No, the driver can call me one."

Oswald asks to be taken to 500 N. Beckley. Whaley begins driving, notices the police sirens and asks "I wonder what the hell is the uproar." Oswald says nothing. Whaley pulls up to 500 N. Beckley, heading south, and parks. Oswald leaves and Whaley doesn't notice which way he walks. Whaley remembers that Oswald was wearing a bracelet on his left arm, which looked like an identification bracelet of some kind. Whaley estimates the distance traveled as 2.5 miles, at a cost of 95 cents. Cannot tell how much time elapsed during the trip, but later when reproducing the trip with a police officer the trip is timed at 9 minutes. Identifies

Oswald's shirt when it is shown to him by Mr. Ball of the Commission.

Whaley recognizes Oswald as his passenger when he sees Oswald's picture in the newspaper. He tells his superiors the next day, who call the police. Whaley is taken to the Dallas police station on the 23rd where he meets with Dallas County Assistant District Attorney Bill Alexander and "two or three who were FBI men," all of whom take his deposition. Whaley is taken to a lineup of suspects downstairs. He is shown "six men, young teenagers, and they were all handcuffed together." Oswald is wearing black pants and white t-shirt, and Oswald is yelling at the policemen, complaining about being put on display with these younger men. Whaley easily identifies Oswald because of his behavior and his age when compared to the teenagers.

Whaley says when Oswald entered the cab he "Wasn't in any hurry. He wasn't nervous or anything." He didn't run, and his clothes were dirty as if he'd slept in them.

CD 87 – Cab stand at Jackson and Lamar to 500 Beckley, estimated 35 mph. 2.6 miles. TIME 7:00 minutes.

Fritz's "Interrogation" from Nov. 22, 10:35 AM: "One of the officers had told me that a cab driver, William Wayne Whaley, thought he had recognized Oswald's picture as the man who had gotten in his cab near the bus station and rode to Beckley Avenue. I asked Oswald if he had ridden a cab on that day, and he said, 'Yes, I did ride in the cab. The bus I got on near work got into heavy traffic and was traveling too slow, and I got off and caught a cab.' I asked him about his conversation with the cab driver, and he remembered that when he got in the cab a lady came up who also wanted a cab, and he told Oswald to tell the lady to 'take another cab.'"

Kelley's "First Interview of Lee Harvey Oswald": "Fritz asked him if he had ridden a taxi that day and Oswald then changed his story and said that when he got on the bus he found that it was going too slow and after two blocks he got off the bus and took a cab to his home; that he passed the time with the cab driver and that the cab driver had told him the President was shot. He paid a cab fair of 85 cents. In response to questions, he said that this was the first time he had ever ridden a cab since a bus was always available."

From CE 2593- Letter from FBI to Commission dated August 21, 1963: "Mileage from cab stand, Greyhound Bus Station, on Lamar between Jackson and Commerce to the intersection of Beckley and Neeley Streets is 2.5 miles. The following route was used for measurement: Lamar south to Jackson, west on Jackson to Austin, south on Austin to Wood, west on Wood to Houston, south and southwest on Houston to Beckley, south on Beckley to Neeley."

12:48 – Police Transcripts

Dispatcher– Signal 19 (shooting) involving the President – suspect white male, 30, slender build, 5 feet 10 inches, 165 pounds, believed to have used a .30 caliber rifle, believed to be in School Book Depository Building, Elm and Houston at this time. 12:48.

Captain C.E. Talbert – 15's at the scene. The building is the old Purse Company at the east side of Houston. Have that cut off on the back side, will you? Make sure nobody leaves there.

Unknown – Any clothing description?

Dispatcher – No clothing description. A white male approximately 30, slender build, 5'10", weight 165.

Talbert – Could 9 (Sawyer) determine whether man was supposed to have been still in the building or was he supposed to have left?

Dispatcher- I didn't know for sure and the witnesses didn't have the description but we have got that building [sic] by now and we should have something before long.

Sawyer- On this building, it's unknown whether he is still in the building or not known if he was there in the first place.

Sgt. G.D. Henslee – Well, all the information we have received, 9 indicates that it did come from the 5th or 4th floor of that building.

Deputy Chief of Police George L. Lumpkin (5) – What building?

Dispatcher- The Texas School Book and Depository building, 5, at Elm and Houston.

Note – At this time, roughly 12:50, Truly clearly hasn't told officers that Oswald is missing yet. Officers still do not have any idea who the suspect is or where he (or they) could be. See 1:25 below. Also note that the initial descriptions of Oswald do not include clothing, but they consist entirely of oddly specific height, weight and age. This description, we are led to believe, comes entirely from Howard Brennan, who saw the shooter from the ground, 90 yards away. If indeed Oswald was a patsy, as he said he was, it would make sense for the 12:44 description not to include clothing, since those who framed him probably would not know what he would be wearing that day.

12:49 – Reporters at Parkland Hospital note that two priests have entered the building (Bishop).

12:50- According to Manchester, "Secret Service Agent Sorrels finds rear door of Depository unguarded by police; asks Truly to draw up a list of his employees."

12:52 – Bugliosi has Oswald leaving the taxi here, two minutes earlier than established tradition.

12:52 - Joesten believes Oswald could not have gotten in the taxi until this time.

12:54- Police Transcripts

Dispatcher to Patrolman JD Tippit - You are in the Oak Cliff area, are you not?

Tippit- Lancaster and 8th.

Dispatcher – You will be at large for any emergency that comes in.

Tippit- 10-4.

Talbert – 15 (Sgt. Jennings) has got about six men checking out that railroad yard, back toward that direction. If you get any information on the shooting...(Garbled)

260 (Harkness) – Give us 508 (crime laboratory station wagon, W.E. Barnes) down to the Texas School Book Depository...It will be a hard one to search out thoroughly without those dogs.

Talbert – I think 5 (Deputy Chief George L. Lumpkin) and 9 (Inspector J.H. Sawyer) both are in the building.

Dispatcher – 78 (Tippit) location... (CD 1420)

Tippit never communicates with the dispatcher, or anyone else, between his last dispatch at 12:54 and the time of his death, presumably at 1:15. He does not tell the dispatcher that he is pursuing a suspect who looks like the President's killer. Tippit, like all other officers, had no idea that the suspect was Oswald, or that Oswald had left the TSBD. He had only received the description that went out at 12:45, 12:48, and 12:55. (See 1:08 below.)

12:54- FBI Interview with Calvin B. Owens, Dallas Police Department (March 17, 1964): "On November 22, 1963, TIPPIT was assigned, alone, to patrol District 78, which bordered by the Trinity River on the east and northeast, Southerland Avenue on the northwest, Sunnyvale and Dante Streets on the west, and Loop 13 or Ledbetter on the south. Sergeant Owens explained that assignment of an officer to an area does not restrict them to that area, in cases of emergency, and due to the extreme emergency of November 22, 1963, numerous patrol units were assigned to different areas. Sergeant Owens cited, for example, that units assigned to districts 95 and 51 had been sent to the downtown area of Dallas immediately after the shooting of President Kennedy. According to Sergeant Owens, Officer Tippit had gone home to eat lunch, which was a normal and approved procedure, at about noontime. Sergeant Owens advised he could not furnish any information as to when or how Tippit's assignment from District 78 had changed as he, Owens, had gone to lunch and had not returned during the time that Tippit's assignment had changed. Tippit had been assigned to district 78 for about six months to a year and had been previously assigned to patrol districts 83 and 84 for three years. His assignment in each case was to patrol the area."

12:54- Oswald gets out of the cab on the 500 block of N. Beckley (CE 1120) His apartment is at 1026 N. Beckley. This time is echoed by Manchester.

CE 1987- "The distance from the 500 block of North Beckley to the 1026 North Beckley, 4/10 of a mile, was walked by SA Barrett in six minutes."

12:55 – The dispatcher repeats the physical description given out at 12:45 and 12:48.

12:55-1:00 – McBride claims that Tippit pulls over an insurance executive named James Andrews on the 300 block of West Tenth street. Tippit looks into Andrews's car and quickly speeds away.

12:58 – Again, Bugliosi places Oswald in the rooming house two minutes earlier than the Warren Commission's official time. Bugliosi's version of the rooming house visit is the quickest and earliest of any other researcher. In this version, Oswald is in the rooming house "just long enough to get his revolver and jacket," and he is outside by 1:00. Although Bugliosi believes Oswald indeed was waiting for the bus, he believes he did not get on it, since it was going in the opposite direction of the Tippit killing. Why Oswald chose to walk in the opposite direction is not explained by Bugliosi. Clearly, Bugliosi wants to give Oswald enough time to get to the Tippit site by 1:08, when he believes the confrontation occurred. Eight minutes, however, is shorter than even the Warren Commission's time for travel from 1026 N. Beckley to Patton and 10th, which is at least ten minutes.

1:00- JFK is pronounced dead by Dr. Kemp Clark at Parkland Hospital (Manchester).

1:00 - The movie starts in the Texas Theater at this time, according to moviegoer George Applin (CD 206).

1:00 –John Gibson (according to WC testimony, volume 7) sits down at the Texas Theater. The Warren Commission's estimate for Oswald entering the theater is 1:40. WC assistant counsel Joseph Ball, in a useless line of questioning, asks several questions about where Gibson was sitting in the theater, what time he *usually* went to the theater on Fridays (not what time he went on that particular Friday), and the unbelievable next question: "Did you see the lights come on in that theater?" Gibson answers "Yes." There is no effort on the part of the Commission to figure out when the lights came on, or even how much time transpired in between Gibson's arrival and the entrance of the police (which supposedly was 40 minutes), or *if Gibson noticed Oswald entering the theater, and if so, when he entered*. Gibson testifies that he sat at "the first chair from the rear on the far right-hand side." He does not notice anybody else in the theater. One wonders why he did not notice Oswald, who was sitting 6 or 7 rows down from the rear, considering that Oswald supposedly entered quickly, suspiciously, and without paying, presumably after the film started (according to Johnny Brewer's testimony). The Warren Commission's lack of interest in Oswald's entrance time at the Texas Theater simply cannot be an accident, seeing as how important it is to the investigation (see the testimonies of Johnny Brewer, Butch Burroughs and Julia Postal below).

After the lights come on in the theater, other audience members start getting up and leaving the theater, asking what is happening. Gibson goes into the lobby and is confronted by two or three police officers. One of the officers, with a shotgun, asks if there is anybody in the balcony. Gibson says he does not know. There are at least six or possibly more policemen downstairs, and "the rest of them" are going upstairs. Gibson goes back into the theater and witnesses as the policemen, six or eight of them, start walking up and down the aisles. Suddenly Oswald is standing up in the center of the aisle holding a gun. Gibson witnesses the confrontation and the arrest, and hears Oswald say, "I protest police brutality" as he is being taken away.

When asked if one group of police headed for Oswald, Gibson says that a boy named Johnny Pardis had followed Oswald into the theater and saw him go upstairs, and that was why the majority of the police were on the balcony, while only 6 or 8 were downstairs. It remains unclear why so many officers were searching the balcony, when no one testifies to seeing Oswald going there.

The above testimony, and all others concerning the capture at the Texas Theater, indicate that the Warren Commission purposely avoided investigating a hugely important fact, namely *when Oswald entered the theater.* There is simply no way that multiple members of the Commission *forgot* to ask multiple witnesses when he entered the theater.

1:00 (CD 677)– At Parkland Hospital, ASAIC Kellerman is informed of the death of the President by Dr. Burkley. Members of the President's staff notify Vice President

Johnson of the death of the President in the presence of SS Agents Kellerman, Youngblood, and Kivett.

1:00 – While reporting live on air in Dealey Plaza for radio station KLRD, reporter Joe Scott says that Officer Gerald Hill has just leaned out of the 4th floor window at the TSBD to tell officers below that four bullet shells have been found on the 4th floor and to tell police to call the Dallas Crime Lab. "Four shells" is repeated several times on air, and later Dan Rather says the shells were found on the 5th floor. The fourth shell will strangely disappear in later reports, and the Warren Commission will have no idea that it ever existed. (The three shells will of course be transferred to the 6th floor.)

1:00- KLRD reports on the radio that a 25-year-old man has been arrested at Elm and Field Streets. He is not a TSBD employee but he claims to have used the bathroom in the TSBD. This is definitely not Oswald, and it is unclear who it is, but later radio reports seem to confuse the two people.

1:00- Oswald is at his rooming house, 1026 N. Beckley Ave (CE 1120).

Oswald tells Captain Fritz and FBI Agents James Hosty, and James Boohkout that he "went home by bus and changed his clothes and went to a movie. Oswald admitted to carrying a pistol with him to this movie stating he did this because he felt like it, giving no other reason" (From FBI Report of 11/23, Appendix XI of the Warren Report).

From Earlene Roberts's Affidavit of December 5, 1963 (WC V. 7): Oswald enters his rooming house without a jacket. He is in the house for a very few minutes, and puts on a dark jacket with a zipper. (She probably mistook his dark overshirt for a jacket.) He leaves the house and waits at the bus stop on the street.

Note: The fact that this testimony is less than two weeks after the event suggests that her recollection that he was waiting for the bus is probably reliable. It is also hard to imagine Oswald making it to the scene of the Tippit murder, 8/10 of a mile away (a brisk 10-12 minute walk according to the FBI), at about 1:14, the latest possible time for the Tippit shooting. Oswald should not have been waiting calmly for a bus – he should have been walking briskly away from the apartment if he was to make his appointment with Tippit.

It should be noted that neither the owner of the building, Gladys Johnson, nor Earlene Roberts (the housekeeper), knew that Oswald owned the .38 Smith and Wesson that he ostensibly used to shoot Tippit and then took to the Texas Theater. Additionally, Roberts did not see him with a gun at any time when he came home at 1:00. According to Johnson's WC testimony, she was present the afternoon of the 22nd when the police entered Oswald's room. She saw them throw a pistol holster down on the bed, which they "took out of one of the drawers of his chest."

From "Leftist Accused," *NY Times* Nov. 22: "A housekeeper at Oswald's rooming house said the young man entered his room shortly after the shooting of the president, got a coat, and went back out. The housekeeper, Mrs. Earlene Roberts, said: 'He came in in a hurry in his shirt sleeves and I said, "Oh, you're in a hurry," and he didn't say anything. He went on in his room and got a coat and put it on. He went out to the bus stop and that's the last I saw of him.' Mrs. Roberts said Oswald rushed into the rooming house, at 1026

North Beckley Road in suburban Oak Cliff. This was shortly after Mrs. Roberts learned, in a telephone call to a friend, that the president had been shot. She said she had not connected Oswald's appearance with the shooting. She described Oswald, who had live in the house since the end of October, as quiet."

From CD 5, in report written by FBI Special Agents Will Griffin and James Kennedy on December 9, 1963: "Mrs. Earlene Roberts, 1026 Beckley, Dallas, Texas, advised she could not furnish the exact time that Oswald returned to his room at 1026 Beckley after the assassination of the President but said a rough guess would be 1 P.M. Mrs. Roberts received a telephone call from a friend telling her the President had just been shot, and Mrs. Roberts turned on the television and recalled the announcer saying that President Kennedy had just been shot and was at Parkland Hospital. Mrs. Roberts advised after Oswald had entered his room at about 1 P.M., on November 22, 1963, she looked out the window and saw Police Car No. 207 with two uniformed policemen in the car which slowed up and stopped in front of the residence at 1026 Beckley, and one of the officers blew the horn on the car and then drove slowly on Beckley toward Zangs Boulevard. Mrs. Roberts said the reason she recalled the number of the car was because she had worked for two policemen who drove squad car 170, and she looked to see if these were the two officers she knew parked in front of the residence.

From CE 2645, FBI report of June 15, 1964 concerning whereabouts of police cars subsequent to the assassination: Dallas Police Officer Jimmy Valentine claims to have been assigned to District 104 and driving police car 207 on November 22. He states that he heard of the assassination at 12:45 and went immediately to the TSBD, staying there until 4:00 or 4:30. He states that at no time did anyone else use his car on that day, and that he did not know Earlene Roberts or Oswald, and that he did not ever drive to 1026 N. Beckley on that day. According to the report, no officers drove past the rooming house at 1026 N. Beckley at 1:00.

As we see, some elements of Earlene Roberts's testimony were accepted by the Warren Commission (The 1:00-1:03 time frame, the fact that he was surly and in a hurry) while others were simply ignored (the dark jacket, waiting for the bus, and the police car honking outside the house).

1:00 – 27-year-old Domingo Benavides witnesses someone, who for several reasons cannot possibly be Oswald, kill Officer Tippit. He vaguely gives the time of 1:00 for the Tippit shooting in his WC testimony (V. 6). Benavides is driving west down 10th street between Marsalis and Denver when he sees Tippit driving his car east on 10th. He then sees the officer standing by the door. He sees "Oswald, or the man who shot him," standing on the other side of the car. He hears three gunshots. After the first shot he pulls his car over and stops it at the curb. He is about a car length away from the police car at the time of the shooting- "a car length east of the front side of it." He sees the shooter walk five feet to the curb, throw the two shells onto the ground, and walk south on Patton Street. Benavides waits for a few minutes, then goes up to the policeman. He uses Tippit's radio to tell the dispatcher that a police officer has been shot. Another passerby sits in the police car and speaks to the police. The dispatcher tells the passerby to get off the radio, that he already knows about the shooting, and to keep the line clear. Benavides leaves the crime scene and walks to his mother's house which is close by. When asked by the Commission if the shooter was reloading his gun, Benavides says he didn't see this, but the shooter was acting like he was going to reload it. Benavides states that he returned to the crime scene after walking to his mother's house. He finds the two bullet shells and picks one up, then drops it on the ground and uses a stick to place them both in a cigarette box. He describes the shooter to the Commission as 5'10", medium weight, "dark...I mean not dark" hair, darker than average skin color, curlier hair than Mr. Belin (his WC interviewer), age around 24-25, wearing a light beige zipper-type jacket, and dark trousers. He does not go to the police station and never identifies Oswald as the shooter. The timing and the physical description rule out Oswald as the killer in Benavides's testimony.

1:00 (estimated)- According to McBride, Tippit enters Top Ten Records at 338 West Jefferson Boulevard and uses the phone. The owners of the record store, who knew Tippit, claimed that Tippit entered in a hurry, spoke to someone briefly on the phone, and then left in a panic, heading west on Jefferson. The record store is seven blocks from the site of Tippit's murder. McBride believes Tippit was desperately looking for Oswald, per instructions. The question remains how he received these instructions, since he could not have received them on the police radio.

1:00- Oswald arrives at his rooming house, "unresponsive to housekeeper's greetings" (Manchester).

1:00-1:03 – Oswald changes his clothes. According to the Dallas PD's timeline of Nov. 22, Detective Boyd later finds five live rounds of .38 caliber ammo in Oswald's left front pocket and Detective Sims finds the bus transfer in Oswald's shirt pocket. Oswald brings his .38 Smith and Wesson with him as well, but there is no way of knowing where he is carrying it when he leaves the house. All of this suggests that Oswald wasn't in the hurry that *Life Magazine* claims he was. He was deliberately changing out of his dirty clothes and into clean ones, and he remembered his wallet and his bus transfer. It is also hard to imagine an agitated, nervous Oswald (who has just killed the president) caring that his clothes were dirty – unless he wanted to disguise himself with the new clothes, which could suggest that he wanted to evade authorities. Nevertheless, the possibility that he ignored his landlord (a smoking gun for Manchester and others); he brought a gun to a movie theater; he appeared to be in a hurry; and he changed his clothes do not mean that he killed the President or J.D. Tippit.

Fritz's "Interrogation," Nov. 22, 10:35 AM: "During this conversation he told me he reached his home by cab and changed both his shirt and trousers before going to the show. He said his cab fair home was 85 cents. When asked what he did with his clothing he took when he got home, he said he put them in the dirty clothes."

Thomas Kelley's "First Interview with Lee Harvey Oswald": "He said he went home, changed his trousers and shirt, put his shirt in a drawer. This was a red shirt, and he put it with his dirty clothes. He described the shirt as having a button down collar and of reddish color. The trousers were grey colored."

1:03- Oswald leaves rooming house (CE 1120). Evidence of this comes only from Earlene Roberts, who was by no means certain of when he came and left. His three minute sojourn at the rooming house must include him putting his clothes in the dirty clothes hamper and remembering (during what would surely be the most exhilarating experience of his life) to bring his wallet and bus transfer. Keep in mind that in interrogation Oswald clearly remembered his whole journey from work to his home and to the theater, including minor details. One would think that he would be too distracted, having just assassinated the President, to remember such things clearly. Jackie Kennedy famously did not remember climbing onto the back of the limousine.

The FBI determines later that Roberts was able to clearly see Oswald standing at the bus stop from her location in the house (CD 1010).

It also must be asked, *If he owned the .38 Smith and Wesson, why did he bring it when he left the house? Was he expecting a confrontation with the police? Was he expecting a confrontation with somebody else? If he did shoot Kennedy, why would he need the Smith and Wesson, when he would be no match for the large police force who would be searching for him? Was it panic that made him bring his gun? If so, why didn't he appear nervous to the majority of people who observed him that day?* If we assume that he did kill Tippit, we must admit that he was clearly not planning to shoot Tippit and could not have expected to see him that day, unless there is something about Oswald and Tippit that we still do not know. According to Jim Bishop, one in five citizens in Dallas in 1963 carried a gun, and it was quite common for young men to bear arms in public.

1:03- *Life* has Oswald "running" out of his apartment after ignoring Roberts's "My, you're sure in a hurry."

1:03 – According to Manchester, Superintendent Truly notices Oswald's absence at the TSBD at this time. He tells a policeman, who attempts unsuccessfully to find Captain Fritz to give him this information.

1:04 – McBride states that Oswald "probably left the rooming house at 1:04," and that the walk to the Tippit murder location is no less than 15 minutes, no matter which route is taken (he himself did the walk many times). McBride also claims that WC investigator David Belin recalled doing the walk in almost 18 minutes, although this was shortened to 11-12 minutes for the official Warren Report. McBride also observes that no witnesses saw Oswald running or walking between his rooming house and the Tippit site.

1:06 – Bugliosi has Deputy Luke Mooney discovering the sniper's nest here, six minutes before Manchester's time. It is indeed strange how early events occur in Bugliosi's timeline compared to other accepted timelines, even those of other "lone nut" theorists like him.

1:06-1:07- Joesten believes Oswald could not have reached his apartment until this time.

1:06-1:07 (WC 3) – Helen Markham is walking south on Patton toward Jefferson on her way to catch the 1:15 bus to work. She arrives at the intersection of 10th and Patton. She sees a man walking away from her, east on 10th street, on the opposite side of the street. Tippit's patrol car approaches the man very slowly from behind. The car stops and the man comes to the driver's side window, and they appear to have a friendly conversation. In "a few minutes" the suspect leaps backward. Tippit calmly exits his car. The suspect walks toward the front of the car and shoots Tippit three times. Tippit falls to the ground and the suspect walks calmly away, fooling with his gun. The suspect stares straight at Markham, then breaks into a trot, running towards Jefferson, holding his gun. Later she says the suspect "wasn't in no hurry" as he left the scene. After the shooting, Markham physically covers her face with her hands out of fear, and is not actually looking at the shooter for a period of time.

Markham tells the Commission that she is a bad judge of distances and cannot accurately tell how far away the suspect was. Markham is the first suspect to arrive at Tippit's body. She is "screaming and hollering" as she tries to save his life. Tippit attempts to speak to her. She refuses to tell the Commission how many feet away the suspect was, because she has no experience measuring feet. She later identifies Oswald as the suspect because his eyes looked wild and glassy. Markham has little memory of the man who arrived next to the scene, but thinks he was in a truck. She does not know if he was the one who radioed the police.

In her comically exasperating testimony, she describes the police lineup at 4:00 of that day (Oswald was #2 in the lineup). Assistant Counsel Joseph Ball asks Markham six times whether she recognized anyone in the lineup, and each time she states emphatically that she did not – that she had never seen any of those men before. Finally she admits that she identified Oswald after repeated questioning, because when she looked at him, she got a chill, and she felt weak. In addition to her problematic WC testimony, Mark Lane writes in *Rush to Judgment* that he interviewed Markham on the phone before her testimony and she stated that Tippit's killer "was a short man, somewhat on the heavy side, with bushy hair." Lane's WC testimony describes this interview. In her own testimony Markham denies ever talking to Mark Lane and denies that the suspect was short, heavyset, with bushy hair (see below, 1:15-1:20).

On the 23rd, Markham told the FBI that the Tippit shooting occurred around 1:30, and that the killer was a white male, about 18 years old, red complexion, black hair, black shoes, tan jacket, and dark trousers (CD 5). This surely does not sound like Oswald, and it is interesting how the jacket becomes gray, white, or tan depending on the witness. In this testimony she says the killer and Tippit had a friendly conversation for about ten seconds while Tippit was in the car and the killer was leaning against the window. After this, Tippit exited the car and was shot *twice* in the head.

Note – Markham's testimony, as well as Officer Leavelle's report in WC Volume 20, suggest that she was highly traumatized even hours after shooting of Tippit, and that her memory of the events was not clear. As Leavelle puts it, later that afternoon at the police station she was still "in shock," and it was "after she recovered" that he brought her to identify Oswald in a lineup at 4:35. Her timing is interesting, in that it places the shooting well before 1:15, which became the WC's official time.

From CE 2180- *Washington Post*, Nov. 26 (transcript of a Dallas PD press conference).

Q- Was he on foot when Tippit saw him?

A- Yes, he was on foot. And apparently headed for the Texas Theater. He then walked across a vacant lot. Witnesses saw him eject the shells from a revolver and place – reload – the gun.

1:07- Oswald enters the Texas Theater, according to a statement by Butch Burroughs in 1991. This obviously makes it impossible for him to have killed Tippit. Burroughs gave this statement in an interview in the History Channel series "The Men Who Killed Kennedy," and it strangely contradicts all his earlier statements to the effect that he did not see Oswald enter the theater at all.

1:08 (CD 728) – Police Transcripts

78 (Tippit) – 78.

15 - 15/2.

Dispatcher - 15/2.

Tippit - 78.

261 – 261.

Dispatcher – 261.

261 – Do you have any clothing description yet?

Dispatcher – All we have is a white male, 30, slender build, 5'10", 165 pounds, armed with a 30 caliber rifle.

1:08 - Interestingly, Bugliosi has Tippit encountering Oswald walking *east* (away from Tippit) at this time (7 minutes earlier than the Warren Report), based on Tippit's failed attempt at contacting the dispatcher (above). He claims Tippit is making this attempt as a response to seeing Oswald, who "vaguely fits the physical description" given out at 12:45, 12:48, and 12:55. Note that the most recent description would have reached Tippit twelve minutes earlier, and it was vague, as Bugliosi admits. Troublingly, this creates a *seven minute* encounter between Oswald and Tippit, if we are to believe the Warren Commission's official timeline in which Tippit is shot at 1:15. Of course, Bugliosi departs from the 1:15 time, and as you will see below, he has Oswald shoot Tippit at 1:11 and escape at 1:12. Bugliosi describes his interview with Jim Bowles, the Dallas PD sheriff who transcribed the police transcripts for the Warren Commission. Bowles speculates that Tippit had been following Oswald for several minutes, from Beckley or Crawford streets, and imagines Oswald walking "like the devil possessed" or "walking too fast, looking over his shoulder, walking in some erratic, jerky way." This, according to Bowles and Bugliosi, constitutes probable cause for Tippit to pull over and talk to Oswald.

Keep in mind: In this scenario Tippit saw "Oswald" from behind, and had heard only the vague physical descriptions from 12:45, 12:48 and 12:55. Also, the suspect was not in the area of downtown, where he was still believed to be hiding. The Tippit shooting was 2.7 miles to the south of Dealey Plaza. Tippit, who was clearly familiar with Dallas, could not have reasonably expected this to be the suspect in the shooting of Kennedy, and he must have wondered why he was given such an unproductive duty, so far from the obvious location of interest, when there were no reports of the suspect being in Oak Cliff. Tippit could not have suspected "Oswald" of escaping from the scene of the crime – he was walking east or west, 2.7

miles to the south of the crime scene, and there is no evidence that "Oswald" was openly brandishing firearms, especially the 30 caliber rifle described at 1:08. So the reason for Tippit to stop this man is still a mystery. And needless to say, it remains a mystery why the dispatcher did not respond to Tippit, or what exactly Tippit was trying to say to him.

1:08-1:09- Oswald leaves his apartment and waits for the bus outside his house, according to Joesten.

1:10 – Radio station WBAP reports that Dallas police have arrested a neatly dressed white man in Dealey Plaza in connection with the shooting. This man is in his early 20's, proclaiming his innocence. WBAP also reports that witnesses saw snipers in 2nd and 4th floor windows of TSBD and that both windows have unobstructed views of the motorcade.

1:10 - Tippit murder witness T.F. Bowley says that Tippit had been killed by this time. In his Dallas County affidavit of December 2, Bowley describes driving west on Jefferson and coming upon the murder site. He sees Tippit lying by the left front wheel of his car. Several people have already gathered. Bowley looks at his watch (the only Tippit witness who claims to have looked at a watch) and sees that it is 1:10. Tippit seems beyond help to Bowley. Bowley finds a man in the car trying to operate the radio (Domingo Benavides, according to all sources). Bowley knows how to operate the radio and uses it to notify the dispatcher that Tippit has been shot. A few minutes later an ambulance arrives and takes the body away.

Obviously this places Tippit's murder at a time that makes it impossible for Oswald to be the killer; the murder itself had already been done and the killer had vanished by 1:10. Interestingly, Bugliosi believes this. But if Oswald left his room at 1:03, and the murder happened several minutes before 1:10, Oswald simply did not shoot Tippit (given the 10 or 15-minute walking time from Oswald's apartment to the Tippit murder site).

In an interview with Joseph McBride, Bowley recalled that he didn't see the killer at any time.

Bugliosi moves Bowley's experience to 1:17, without any explanation.

1:11- Police Transcripts

Inspector J.H. Sawyer (9)– On the 3rd floor of this book company down here, we found empty rifle hulls and it looked like the man had been here for some time. We are checking it out now.

1:11 – According to Bugliosi, William Scoggins observes Tippit stop and talk to "Oswald" at this time. This timing is quite arbitrary, considering the vagueness of Scoggins's WC testimony (see 1:15-1:20 below). He also places Benavides's and Markham's observations at this time.

1:12- Manchester has Deputy Sheriff Luke Mooney finding the three empty cartridges on the 6th floor at this time.

1:12 – Bugliosi has Oswald leaving the Tippit scene at this time, and running south on Patton, cutting across the yard of Barbara and Virginia Davis. Bugliosi's timing gives Oswald 24 minutes to reach the Texas Theater, only 6/10 of a mile away.

Inspector Sawyer to dispatcher: We have found empty rifle hulls on the 3rd/5th floor and it appears the suspect was there for some time.

1:12 – (WC Testimony, volume 4) Lieutenant J.C. Day, crime scene investigator with 23 years of experience with the Dallas Police Department, arrives at the TSBD after receiving a call from the dispatched to go to 411 Elm St. He is greeted at the front door by Lt. Sawyer and is directed to go to the 6th floor. He takes the stairs because none of the officers can figure out how to operate the elevators. He goes to the southeast corner of the building (mistakenly refers to the "northeast corner" twice) where some bullet hulls have been found. When he first arrives at the scene on November 22, there is a pop bottle, a sack, and a paper bag next to the three hulls. The paper bag is between the pipe and the wall and is later given to the FBI with the rifle. This is the bag that Oswald is alleged to have used to carry the gun to work. The sack contains chicken bones, which Day throws away. The pop bottle does not contain Oswald's fingerprints. One of the other TSBD workers states that someone else had been eating lunch in that location, and Day assumes the objects have nothing to do with Oswald. *Note: Strangely, this places Bonnie Ray Williams in the sniper's nest, since the chicken lunch and the Dr. Pepper were admittedly his. Since Williams was there until 12:15 or 12:20, it is hard to imagine anyone actually using the sniper's nest to kill the president.* Day does not find fingerprints on the sack when he gives them to the FBI, but when the sack is returned to him on Nov. 24, there is a fingerprint.

Lt. Day directs one of his officers, R.L. Studebaker, to take photos of the hulls in the locations they were before they were moved. He tells the WC that the photo of Exhibit 482, which was taken off the outside of the 6th floor TSBD less than a minute after the shooting (by a "news photographer"), shows a box that was not there when he arrived, and does not appear in the photos of the inside of the 6th floor in the photos in Exhibits 715-716. Day states, "I still don't quite understand that one in relation to pictures here unless something was moved after this one was taken before I got there." Day processes the three hulls for fingerprints and does not find any. Captain Fritz tells Day to come to the northwest corner of the building where the rifle has been found.

Lieutenant Day cannot make positive identification of the prints, but tells the Commission that he thinks they belonged to Oswald, because there were palm and fingerprints of Oswald in Captain Fritz's office. It is 11:45 on November 22 when Day releases the rifle to the FBI. *Note: Sebastian Latona, the FBI's fingerprint expert, received the rifle after Day released it and found no print whatsoever. According to Latona, the FBI's Dallas office sent the Dallas PD's original lift to FBI headquarters on November 29. Latona identified this lift as belonging to Oswald (described in depth in Latona's WC testimony). The FBI's Gemberling Report of Nov. 30 does not refer to palm prints on the rifle, and connection of the rifle to Oswald is based on handwriting evidence on the order form.*

Day states that by November 25, when the photo of Exhibit 726 was taken, there had been some movement of the boxes on the 6th floor by the window.

Day finds a palm print on one of the boxes by the window. He tears the cardboard off of the box and has it processed. It is found to be Oswald's right hand palm print.

In Oswald's 201 File (Volume 20) an FBI report of December 27 indicates that the paper and tape used to create the paper bag found in the sniper's nest (the bag which is alleged to have carried the rifle) are not identical with the tape and paper used in the depository. This bag was fashioned using materials from outside the building. Additionally, the tape is not identical with tape found in Ruth Paine's home and the bag is not identical with paper used by Oswald as an envelope.

On Nov. 24, the Postal Inspector interviewed Oswald: "He denied emphatically that he had ever ordered a rifle under his name or any other name, nor permitted anyone else to order a rifle to be received in [his post office box]. Further, he denied that he had ordered any rifle by mail order or bought any mail order for the purpose of buying such a rifle. In fact, he claimed he owned no rifle and had not practiced or shot a rifle other than possibly a .22, small bore rifle, since his days with the Marine Corp. He stated that 'How can I afford to order a rifle on my salary of $1.25 an hour when I can't hardly feed myself on what I make.'" (The Warren Commission states that the rifle is supposed to have cost $21.45. This included the scope and the shipping and handling. Both the rifle and scope are alleged by the WC to have been purchased from Klein's Sporting Goods of Chicago. This would cost Oswald at least two days' wages, or 17 hours of labor.) From Oswald 201 File, Volume 20, maryferrell.org.

1:13 (CD 677)– Assistant Press Secretary Malcolm Kilduff enters Lyndon Johnson's hospital room and the two of them decide that news of the President's death will not be released to the press until Johnson is released from the hospital. Mrs. Kennedy and White House staff have already decided to return the President's body to Washington on Air Force One.

1:15 – The box office opens at the Texas Theater; *Cry of Battle* and *War is Hell* are playing. There are 14 customers lined up to buy tickets. Julia Postal begins selling tickets at 90 cents each (Bishop).

1:15- According to the Dallas PD "Report on Events Following the President's Murder" from Nov. 22, Sheriff Mooney finds the empty shells by the southeast window on the 6th floor of the TSBD and notifies Captain Fritz. Detectives Johnson and Montgomery are placed in charge of this area until J.C. Day and Detective Studabaker arrive from the Crime Lab.

Regarding the location of the cartridge cases found at the sniper's nest: In J. Edgar Hoover's letter to Lee Rankin, of March 27 1964 (CD 775), Hoover states that according to FBI tests, when fired at a 45 degree downward angle, the Manlicher-Carcano rifle ejects the bullet cartridges from 55 to 115 inches from the ejection port. After striking the floor, the cartridges can ricochet up to 10 feet in any direction. Contrast this to the proximity of the three cartridges to the open window in the sniper's nest, as seen in the photos from CD 87. According to typical cartridge ejection distances, the cartridges should have been nowhere near the sniper's nest.

1:15-1:20

CD 87- "Witnesses stated that Oswald had been walking along west on the south side of 10th street when Officer Tippit, driving east on 10th Street, pulled alongside and spoke to him. Oswald leaned on the open window of the stopped police car and said something to the officer. The officer then left the cruiser, using the left door, and started walking toward Oswald by walking around the front of the police car. Oswald had backed away from the cruiser and was standing near the sidewalk. As the officer rounded the left front fender of the police car, Oswald fired three shots. Shot once in the head, twice in the chest, Officer Tippit fell to the ground, mortally wounded, and never regained consciousness. Oswald turned, ran, and was observed by witnesses continuing west between Jefferson and 10th streets."

The Warren Report changes the direction of Oswald's walk on 10th street, and in the official version he is walking *east*, away from Tippit. This of course makes it less likely that Tippit identified him as the killer of JFK, based on the vague description given out at 12:55, and does not answer the question of where Oswald was going. If "Oswald" was indeed walking east, he was walking away from his final destination of the Texas Theater, and after shooting Tippit, ran the opposite direction that he'd been going. Presumably, he was in a state of panic and madness.

From FBI report, 11/23, Appendix XI of Warren Report: "Oswald frantically denied shooting police officer Tippit or shooting President John F. Kennedy."

(WC V. 3) Taxi driver William Scoggins, 49, has discharged a passenger at 321 N. Ewing at 1:00. He goes to get his lunch at the Gentlemen's Club at 125 Patton, where he stays for "10, 12, Or 15 minutes," and hears from another patron that the President has been shot. He goes out to his car to eat his lunch. He is parked at the corner of Patton and 10th facing north. He sees a police car "cruising east there on 10th street," traveling no more than 10 or 12 miles an hour. He is eating a sandwich and drinking a Coke. He sees the police car stop next to a man wearing a light colored jacket. The man appears to be a little east, or standing at the front of the police car. The man is on the sidewalk and has been walking *west* on 10th street, toward Tippit. Scoggins cannot see the man's face. He sees the police officer get out of the car and take a step. Scoggins begins to eat his sandwich, and then hears three or four gunshots, "fast." He sees the police officer grab his stomach and fall.

Scoggins begins to get out of his cab but hides when he sees the man "coming round." The man cuts across a yard and runs into some bushes, then goes south down Patton. Scoggins sees the shooter look left over his shoulder as he flees, "kind of loping, trotting." He holds a pistol in his left hand and says "something like, 'Poor damn cop,' or 'Poor dumb cop.'" Two days later Scoggins will the FBI that he cannot identify this man as Oswald (CD 5). After the killer flees, Scoggins radios his dispatcher and says that a police officer has been shot at 10th and Patton, and asks for an ambulance. He says the ambulance "was already a block and quarter from the scene," so they arrive quickly.

By the time Scoggins goes up to see the victim, the ambulance has already arrived and the body is being put onto a stretcher. The body has fallen "by the side of the front...a little bit forward of the door." He states that the office fell forward, "in a crumpled manner."

Scoggins does not know if the ambulance arrived as a result of his call – "They got there awfully quickly if they did." As Scoggins is standing by Tippit's police car, he sees that Tippit's gun is on the ground, "like kind of under his body when they picked him up." A man picks up the gun and says, "Let's go see if we can find him." (This is used-car salesman Ted Callaway.) Scoggins thinks this man is a "kind of police, a Secret Service or something." He drives the man all over the neighborhood, looking for the suspect, and does not remember the route they took. Scoggins says, "I still thought he was connected with the police department in some way." They drive around asking people if they have seen the suspect.

According to Attorney Mark Lane's testimony to the Warren Commission, and based on a conversation he had with Helen Markham in late February or early March 1964: "The affidavit in the district attorney's office indicates that a person saw a stopped police car, walked up to the police car, leaned on it with his arms on the window, or what would be a window sill or window ledge of the automobile, and then stepped back a step or two, the officer came out, and the person shot Officer Tippit to death.

"The affidavit is peculiarly sparse in reference to the assailant, the man who killed Tippit, by an eyewitness who said she was just 50 feet away.

"Her description of this person is found in two different portions of the affidavit- he was young, white, male, and that is the entire description present in the affidavit at that time.

"I spoke with the deponent, the eyewitness, Helen Louise Markham, and [she] told me she was a hundred feet away from the police car, not the 50 feet which appears in the affidavit. She gave to me a more detailed description of the man who she said shot Officer Tippit. She said he was short, a little bit on the heavy side, and his hair was somewhat bushy. I think it is fair to state that an accurate description of Oswald would be average height, quite slender, with thin and receding hair" (WC V. 2).

From "Note from J.W. Fritz to Jesse Curry of 23 December 1963": "The two .38 cartridge cases were found by Barbara Jeanette Davis and Virginia Davis in front of their home, 400 E. Tenth Street, where they had seen Oswald throw them as he was reloading his gun. Four bullets were recovered from Officer Tippit's body and they were of the same caliber as the gun Oswald was arrested with."

CE 1987- "The distance from 1026 North Beckley to the location in the 400 block of East 10th street where Police Officer J.D. Tippit was shot and killed on November 22, 1963, 8/10 of a mile, was walked by SA Barrett in 12 minutes."

Unknown time – Mrs. Barbara Jeanette Davis (WC testimony) is lying in bed at her home at 410 E. 10th Street when she hears two gunshots. She gets out of bed and puts her shoes on. At first, she doesn't go outside. Then she goes to the door and holds the screen open. She first sees Helen Markham screaming over the body of the policeman in the street, and then sees the suspect walking across her yard. He is holding a gun and looks like he is emptying it into the palm of his left hand. He looks at her and smiles, then walks around the corner at a normal pace. She does not see him throw anything away. She goes inside and calls the police, telling them that a police officer has been shot. Then she goes outside and approaches the dead policeman in the street. She is in the street "not five minutes" when the police arrive, so she goes back to her house. She later finds the bullet shell in the grass beside the house. Later that afternoon her sister-in-law finds another shell in the yard.

Note – Google Maps lists the distance from 1026 N. Beckley to 400 E. 10th Street as 0.8 miles, with the walking time between the two locations as 16 minutes. If Oswald left the rooming house at 1:03, this would put him at the location at 1:19, four minutes after he was supposed to have shot Tippit (at the latest estimate). Three different routes give the same approximate walking time. Considering that the shooting is reported by the citizen using Tippit's radio at 1:16, the confrontation and the shooting (and the suspect's flight) must have occurred around one or two minutes earlier (if we ignore Bowley's seemingly clearheaded testimony). We can place Tippit's actual murder at around 1:14 at the latest, if the police dispatch time is accurate, but before 1:10 if Bowley's testimony is accurate. Oddly, few of the witnesses are asked by the Warren Commission what time the murder occurred, and when they are, witnesses are unable to answer.

The only witness who places the killer as walking east, with his back to Tippit, is Helen Markham. Scoggins has the killer walking west, facing Tippit. In CD 87, the FBI has Oswald walking west, approaching Tippit. If Oswald was on his way from his apartment to the Texas Theater when he killed J.D. Tippit, it is hard to understand why he was walking west on 10th street at Patton. He had gone out of his way in some kind of loop for no apparent reason, and then decided at some point during his walk to head toward the theater. If he had just walked straight down Beckley and turned right on Jefferson he would've arrived at the theater quicker. But instead he went south of his apartment and ended up to the east of Beckley, heading west. Where was Oswald coming from? If he was walking west, in the general direction of the theater, several questions arise. Where had he been? Why did he travel east and south, and then change directions and decide to go west towards the theater? If he was panicking after shooting the president, this might be believable – but the more circuitous his route was, the longer it would take him, and the more unlikely it is that Oswald could arrive in ten minutes or less.

If he was walking east, as Markham says, we must wonder where he was going, and it was clearly away from the Texas Theater. And we must remember that Markham, by all accounts, was hysterical at the time of the shooting and for several hours afterward.

We must also remember that Earlene Roberts saw Oswald waiting for the bus outside the rooming house. We don't know how long he was there, but it just doesn't give him enough time to get to the Tippit site, even by 1:14, the latest possible time for the shooting. With all this, it seems nearly impossible for Oswald to be the killer of Tippit.

From "Leftist Accused, *NY Times* Nov. 22: "The car's driver, Patrolman Tippit, had not made any call that he was going to question anyone. Eight other officers converged on the spot. They found Patrolman Tippit lying on the sidewalk, dead from two .38-caliber bullet wounds. They began a search for nearby buildings for the killer."

At the time of Tippit's murder Acquilla Clemons is working at 327 East 10th, just down the block from the shooting. She hears the shots and runs into the street. She sees a man holding reloading a gun. He is short, chunky and heavy, "wasn't a very big man." She sees another man across the street from the shooter. The man with the gun waves to the other man, who runs off in another direction. The man who did not do the shooting is tall and thin and wears a khaki shirt. Clemons is not interviewed by the Warren Commission. Two days later a man with a gun comes to Clemons's house and says someone might hurt her if she speaks about what she saw, that it would be best if she does not say anything (Interview with Mark Lane, from the film *Rush to Judgment*, 1966).

CE 2593- "Mileage from 1026 North Beckley to 404 East Tenth Street is .9 miles. The following route was used for measurement: South on Beckley from 1025 North Beckley to Davis, east on Davis to Crawford, south on Crawford to Tenth Street, east on Tenth Street to 404 East Tenth."-

From "Note from J.W. Fritz to Jesse Curry of 23 December 1963": "Helen Markham, 328 E. Ninth Street, saw Oswald shoot Officer Tippit and positively identified him in a lineup. Officer Tippit was shot at 1:18 P.M. on November 22, 1963 in front of 400 E. Tenth Street.

Several other witnesses identified him as the man running from the scene and toward the theater."

1:15 – (WC testimony) Ted Callaway, a car salesman at Harris Bros. Auto Sales at 501 East Jefferson, with six years of experience in the Marine Corps, hears five pistol shots in the direction of the Tippit shooting site. He runs to the site, one block away, and sees Scoggins hiding by his taxicab. He sees the shooter run across the Davis's yard and south down Patton. Callaway shouts at the shooter, "Hey man, what the hell is going on?" The shooter utters something incomprehensible, shrugs his shoulders, and continues running. The shooter is carrying his gun in "raised pistol position," as they used to say in the Marine Corps (with the muzzle pointed upward, arm bent at the elbow). The shooter is about 56 feet away from Callaway at the closest. The shooter is wearing dark trousers, a light tannish gray windbreaker jacket, fair complexion, dark hair, 5'10", 160 pounds. Callaway runs to the scene, where he finds Tippit lying on his left side with his pistol underneath him. The pistol is out of its holster, which is unsnapped. An ambulance arrives, and Calloway helps load Tippit in the ambulance. He and Scoggins search the neighborhood in Scoggins's taxicab. They go from 10th to Crawford, Crawford to Jefferson, Jefferson to Beckley, and do not see the assailant. Callaway believes that if they had gone straight down Jefferson they would have seen him, since he ended up at the Texas Theater. Later that night, at the police station, around 6:30 or 7:00, Callaway identifies Oswald as the shooter, from a lineup of four men.

1:15 – Bugliosi has Domingo Benavides approaching Tippit, lying on the ground, at this time.

1:15 – Manchester has Tippit encountering Oswald at this time. Oswald shoots Tippit four times, and is identified by nine people.

1:15- Dr. Earl Rose's autopsy report (written at 3:15 that afternoon at Parkland) provides 1:15 as the time of death for J.D. Tippit. Obviously this presents a problem and could be a mistake. If it is not a mistake, it suggests that the police transcriptions have been falsified (which is very unlikely, since the recordings match the transcripts) and Tippit's killing was much earlier, meaning that Oswald could not have killed Tippit, since he would have been at his rooming house or just leaving it at the time of the murder (texashistory.unt.edu).

Strangely, the 1:15 time of death is echoed by the report of Officers Davenport and Bardin, who specifically state that Tippit died at the hospital at 1:15, and that they observed doctors attempting to revive him. Their statement claims that Dr. Richard Liquori pronounced Tippit dead (Supplementary Offense Report Concerning Shooting of Officer Tippit, texashistory.unt.edu).

1:16- TF Bowley ("Citizen"), using police radio reports a police officer (Tippit) has been shot on 10th street between Marsalis and Beckley

Citizen – Hello, police officer…We've had a shooting down here.

Dispatcher – Where's it at?

Citizen – On 10th street.

Dispatcher – What location on 10th street?

Citizen – Between Marsalis and Beckley. It's a police officer. Somebody shot him...What's this? 404 10th street.

Dispatcher: 78 (Patrolman J.D. Tippit).

Citizen – Hello, police officer, did you get that? 510 East Jefferson.

Regarding the 6 minute delay from Bowley's initial witnessing of Tippit's body (1:10) to his use of the police radio, McBride states that Bowley sat in his car in shock for a few minutes before coming to the aid of Domingo Benavides, who was trying unsuccessfully to operate the radio.

1:16- *Life* names Ted Callaway and Helen Markham as main witnesses to the Tippit killing. Details are similar to their testimonies. Markham sees Oswald with a gray jacket.

Arthur William Smith, 20, is a block east of the Tippit shooting site with his friend Jimmy Burt when he hears gunshots. He looks and sees "Oswald running and policeman falling." He sees the side of the shooter as he runs. Later he sees Oswald on TV and states that Oswald's hair was lighter than it was when he saw him after the shooting (WC 7).

Warren Reynolds, 28, is working at Reynolds Motor Company at 500 East Jefferson when he hears gunshots from the Tippit shooting site, one block away (WC testimony). He goes out onto the porch of his business and sees the shooter walking west down Jefferson with the gun in his hand. He then puts the gun in his pants and continues walking. Reynolds follows the shooter up the street behind the service station and loses him. He assumes the shooter is in the alley. In his own mind he identifies Oswald as the shooter, based on seeing Oswald's face in the media. He is convinced that it was Oswald, "Unless you have somebody who looks an awful lot like him there." He isn't interviewed by authorities until January 21, 1964. On January 23 he is shot in the head with a .22 caliber rifle in the basement of his auto business. He miraculously survives. He tells the Commission that he believes it was retaliation in some way for chasing Oswald and states that there are rumors that he directed the police to the Texas Theater. He has no solid information to support his claim, but he also says that someone attempted to kidnap his 10-year-old daughter three weeks after he got out of the hospital, on February 20. Later someone unscrewed the lightbulb on his front porch.

Reynolds's statement to the FBI on the 22nd of January (CE 2523) is slightly different from his WC testimony above. In the earlier statement, Reynolds sees the individual running south on Patton and walking "at a fast rate of speed west on Jefferson." The individual turns and walks *north* at the Ballew Texaco Service Station (the WC testimony had the suspect going west through the alley in conformity with the WC narrative). He loses site of the individual and the workers at the station tell Reynolds that the suspect went through the parking lot. When shown a photo of Oswald, Reynolds tells the FBI that "he is of the opinion that Oswald is the person he had followed" that day; "however, he would hesitate to definitively identify Oswald as the individual."

Time Unknown: 85 (Walker)- We have a description on this suspect over here last seen on Jefferson. Last seen about the 300 East Jefferson. He's a white male, about 30, 5'8", black hair, slender, wearing a white jacket, white shirt and dark slacks.

Dispatcher – Armed with what?

85- Unknown.

1:16- According to the Warren Report, Oswald walks south on Patton, emptying his gun cartridges on the ground, and runs west on Jefferson. He then goes into the parking lot behind a gas station, throws his white jacket on the ground, and continues down Jefferson toward the Texas Theater.

1:17 or 1:20- Officer McDonald, on his way to the Oak Cliff area (Tippit murder location), hears a description of the suspect: "White male, approximately 27 years old, 5 foot 10, weight about 145 pounds, wearing light clothing" (WC V. 3)

1:18- According to Detective J.R. Leavelle's case report for Oswald's arrest, the Tippit shooting happens at this time. As Leavelle states, "The above defendant was walking west in the 400 blk. of east 10th when stopped by above complainant to be questioned. When Tippit got out of his squad car to further question the defendant, the defendant, Oswald, pulled a .38 pistol and shot officer Tippit three times: one time each in the head, chest, and stomach." Leavelle lists Markham, Scoggins, Sam Guinyard, and Rowley, and the Davis sisters as witnesses to Tippit's killing, and identifies Postal and Brewer as witnesses to Oswald entering the theater. Note that Oswald is walking west, toward Tippit, in this version of events. His brief witness descriptions are similar to witnesses' WC testimonies, but he tends to represent the witnesses as much more certain of Oswald's guilt than they appear on closer scrutiny (texashistory.unt.edu).

1:18- Dispatcher – General Broadcast – All squads, we have a report that an officer has been involved in a shooting 400 E. 10th.

Joseph McBride mentions that the officers, in the recordings, sound remarkably calm, even callous about the killing of Tippit.

According to Tippit's autopsy, there are four bullet wounds. The first is just above his right eye, and the other three are in the chest. The bullet that caused the head wound exited the head. The fourth wound in the chest is superficial and "no missile is present in this area." According to the FBI's analysis of three of these bullets (CD 774), C251 and C253 are copper-coated lead bullets of Winchester-Western manufacture, while C252 is of Remington-Peters manufacture. The FBI is unable to determine whether or not these three bullets were fired from the same weapon. The HSCA later rules that it is inconclusive whether the four bullets that killed Tippit (CE 602-605) were fired from Oswald's revolver (CE 143).

1:18 – Officers Poe and Jez arrive at the Tippit murder scene, according to their Supplementary Offense Report (texashistory.unt.edu). Tippit's body has already been taken from the scene. Poe and Fez speak to Helen Markham, incorrectly named as Helen Marsille in their report. Markham states that Tippit's shooter threatened to kill her when she went to help Tippit (this is not mentioned in any of her testimonies). She describes the killer as 25 years old, 5 feet 10 inches, wearing brown jacket and dark pants. Six or seven witnesses tell officers that the suspect is running west in the alley between 10th and Jefferson.

1:18- Citizen informs dispatcher of Tippit's murder (From CD 290 - Texas Radio Log written by Chief Curry).

Manchester suggests that in Oswald's "epic stupidity" and his panic, "it is highly likely that he lost his head when Officer Tippit beckoned to him..." Unfortunately, Oswald's stupidity and panic are not confirmed by other witnesses on that day. No one other than Johnny Brewer claimed to witness Oswald acting nervously. And while Oswald was probably dyslexic, it is not evident that he was unintelligent. (See Mailer, who believes that Oswald was quite intelligent.)

1:19 – Police Transcripts

Units 85, 602, 19, 531 are en route to "Two different locations, 501 E. Jefferson and 501 E. Tenth."

531 : Suspect is running west on Jefferson from the location - no physical description.

Dispatcher – The suspect's running west on Jefferson from the location.

85 (Patrolman R.W. Walker) – 10-4.

Dispatcher – No physical description.

Citizen – Hello, hello, hello...

602 (Ambulance) – 602.

Citizen - ...from out here on 10th street, 500 block. This police officer's just shot, I think he's dead.

Oswald's journey on Jefferson: Joesten states that Jefferson is a busy thoroughfare full of shops and generally quite crowded in the middle of the day, and that it is hard to imagine Oswald running unnoticed all the way to the Texas Theater.

1:19- According to McBride, the first ambulance, coming from a funeral home two blocks away, arrives at the Tippit site.

1:20 – At the Texas Theater, the main feature (*War is Hell*) starts at this time (George Applin, CD 206).

1:22- Manchester has Oswald cutting through Patton St., running toward West Jefferson Blvd. This is literally at the scene of the Tippit shooting, seven minutes after it has occurred. What has Oswald been doing for 7 minutes, while the police have arrived at the scene? Manchester does not enlighten us. Oswald emerges at a Texaco station on Jefferson and drops his jacket on the ground at this time.

Manchester has a "fresh description" of Oswald being broadcast by police at 1:22, updated by the descriptions of two women. Manchester is probably referring to the description at 1:23, but does not tell us who the two women are, or which crime scene they are from.

1:22 – Police Transcripts

Officer Nelson, who had been ordered to go to Oak Cliff with Tippit, but instead went to Dealey Plaza, radios: "I'm in my car at Elm and Houston. Do you want me over there?" The dispatcher replies, "87, report to 4340 West Davis at the service station for information regarding the suspect on this Signal 19 of the President." McBride questions why Nelson, after obeying these orders, went to Oak Cliff afterwards of his own accord, and in general seemed to operate with autonomy, suffering no reprimands for doing so.

1:22- According to McBride, the first police unit arrives at the Tippit murder site.

1:22- According to Officer Eugene Boone's WC testimony (V.3) this is the time that he finds the rifle in the "northeasterly" corner of the 6th floor TSBD. A newsman is up there with him taking movie film of the rifle at the moment it is discovered. There are discrepancies for the finding of the rifle – who found it, when it was found, and what make and model it was, are unresolved issues, as we will see.

From CE 3048, KBOX audio reel number 1, November 22, 1963, afternoon: "A rifle found in a staircase on the fifth floor of the building on which the assassin is believed to have shot the President of the United States. Sheriff's deputies identify the weapon as a 7.65 Mauser, a German-made rifle with a telescopic sight. It had one shell in its chamber. Three spent shells were found nearby."

According to an FBI interview on the 23rd, Deputy Constable Seymour Weitzman finds the rifle at 1:22 and calls Boone's attention to it. Weitzman describes it as a "7.65 caliber Mauser bolt-action rifle" with a "four-power 18 scope of apparent Japanese manufacture" (CD 5).

1:23 – Police Transcripts

Unknown – What was his direction of travel on Jefferson?

Dispatcher - Traveling west on Jefferson, block. Last seen 401 Jefferson, correction, it will be east.

1:23 – (From WC V. 4) Captain Fritz asks Lt. Day to photograph the rifle before it is moved. The rifle is resting upright in between two rows of boxes, in a space just narrow enough to hold it. Day takes the photo which is Exhibit 719 – the northwest corner of the building where the rifle has been found. (See CE 723, the photo of the sniper's nest in the southeast corner of the TSBD. Note that the gun is found in the opposite corner of the building from sniper's nest). Day picks up the gun and Captain Fritz opens the bolt as Lt. Day holds it. A live round falls out of the gun. Lt. Day process the live round for fingerprints and finds none. Day dusts the bolt for fingerprints and finds none. Day takes the rifle to his office where he dictates to his secretary the information that was "stamped on the scopic sight on top of the gun": "4 x 18, coated, Ordinance Optics, Inc., Hollywood, California, 010 Japan. OSC inside a cloverleaf design." He also dictates to his secretary the following regarding the gun: "When bolt opened one live round was in the barrel. No prints are on the live round. Three spent hulls were found under the window. They were picked up by Detective Sims and witnessed by Lieutenant Day and Studebaker. The clip is stamped, 'SM1, 9 x 2.'" Day sees faint palm prints "near the firing end of the barrel about three inches under the woodstock when I took the woodstock loose." He is about to attempt to process the palm prints using photography when he receives instructions from the chief's office to go no further with the processing, because the FBI is going to complete the investigation. This further confuses the question of *where* the print that implicated Oswald came from.

WBAP reports live on air that J.C. Day presented reporters with a "British 303" rifle from the scene on the 6th floor.

1:24 – Dispatcher describes a white male wanted for murder of police officer, 30 yrs old, 5'8", slender, black hair, white jacket, white shirt, dark trousers, "last seen running west on Jefferson."

1:24 – Police Transcripts (CD 728)

103 to 109 – Any description of him?

103 – Have description of white male, about 30, 5'8", black hair, white jacket. Any units spotting a white station wagon, with license prefix PE, proceed with caution and advise. In area of West Jefferson.

1:25- According to CD 5 (FBI Gemberling Report of November 29), Tippit is pronounced dead at Methodist Hospital at this time. Tippit's shooting is not broadcast to all units by the dispatcher until 1:18, and McBride claims the first ambulance didn't arrive until 1:22. While it is not impossible, it is cutting it close to place Tippit at Methodist Hospital, 1.2 miles away, at 1:25. This means that in seven minutes the ambulance has arrived, the ambulance has taken him to the hospital, doctors have examined him, and he has been pronounced dead on arrival. Below we will see that just one minute later, 1:26, the dispatcher broadcasts news of his death. We know that T.F. Bowley didn't alert the police about Tippit's murder until 1:16. What we are discovering is a timeline that may not be outside of the realm of possibility, but is becoming absurdly compressed; the Keystone Cops come to mind. (One wonders why the body was moved so quickly when it was clear to even the bystander who called the police that Tippit was already dead (as McBride notes, T.F. Bowley was proficient in artificial respiration and knew Tippit was dead as early as 1:10). One would think that for the purposes of the investigation his body would be kept in the place where it fell. If the ambulance were to arrive immediately after the call at 1:16, and the body moved without any hesitation, it may be possible for Tippit to be pronounced dead at 1:25. The autopsy report may have reported his death at 1:15 because that was the time the doctors thought he had been shot on the street.

1:25 – According to one report, Sheriff Weitzman finds the rifle on the 6th floor of the TSBD, 115 feet where the shells are, 5 feet from the west wall and 8 feet from the west stairway (Dallas PD, "Report on Events Following the President's Murder," Nov. 22, texashistory.unt.edu).

1:25 – This is the oddly late, and certainly incorrect, time given for the Tippit shooting by William Scoggins in his interview with FBI Special Agent Louis Kelley on November 23, 1963. Kelley writes: "He had picked up a fair at Love Field on Friday, November 22, 1963, which he discharged at 321 North Ewing at 1 P.M. He then drove to the Gentleman's Club, 125 South Patton, to get a cold drink to go with his lunch. He could not find a parking place in front of the club, so he parked on the east side of Patton at 10th street and stated he parked where a stop sign had been but had been removed. He parked heading north on the right side of the street.

"He walked back to the club, obtained his cold drink, and watched the President on TV for a minute. He then returned to his cab and got his lunch out of the pocket. He estimated this to be about 1:25 P.M.

"About the time he got his lunch out, he saw a policeman in a squad car going east on 10th street at a slow rate of speed. This officer stopped on 10th street just east of Patton. The officer got out of his car and apparently said something to a man walking west on 10th Street and who was on the south side of 10th. When the officer spoke to him, the man stopped.

"The next thing that attracted Scoggins' attention was a gun firing and he heard three or four shots, saw smoke near the squad car and saw the officer fall beside the car on the driver's side. The man the officer stopped started running. He ran west on 10th to Patton and south on Patton to Jefferson. The last time he saw this man was when he was going down Jefferson. He reported this to the dispatcher as soon as the man passed his cab and was asked if an ambulance was needed. He advised the dispatcher he did need an ambulance and shortly thereafter the ambulance arrived as did other officers.

"He stated he did not know the man who shot the officer but would know him if he saw him. He stated this man muttered as he passed his cab 'Poor dumb cop' or 'Poor damn cop.' He was not certain which, and stated that when this man passed his cab, he had a pistol in his left hand."

Note again, Scoggins's insistence that Tippit's shooter was walking west, towards Tippit. The Warren Report officially has the shooter walking away from Tippit.

1:25- Police Transcripts

279 (unknown officer) – We believe that we've got that suspect on shooting that officer out here. We got his

jacket. Believe he dumped it behind a service station at 400 block West Jefferson and he had a white jacket on.

Deputy Chief of Police N.T. Fisher – Is there any indication that it has any connection with this other shooting?

Dispatcher- Well, the descriptions on the suspects are similar and it is possible.

Sergeant Gerald L. Hill - I'm at 12 and Beckley right now – have a man in the car with me that can identify the suspect if anybody gets him, the one.

19 (Sgt. C.B. Owens)- One of the men at the service station that saw him seems to think he is in this block of 400 East Jefferson, behind this service station. Will you get me some more squads out here?

79 (Patrolman Anglin)- En route.

1:26- Dispatcher states that Tippit has been pronounced DOA at Methodist Hospital

Dispatcher – 87 (Nelson).

Nelson – A white station wagon believed to be PE3435, unknown make and [ ] late model, occupied by two white males left this fellow's station going east on Davis and believed to have a shotgun or rifle laying in back seat.

According to William Weston's analysis of the period in between the finding of the jacket behind the service station at 1:25 and the finding of the suspect in the library at 1:35, there was a deliberate reluctance of the police to search the actual parking lot where the jacket was found. The police searched several vacant buildings and a church rather than the lot itself, and then rushed to the library, which in Weston's belief shows explicit orders from on high to let the suspect hiding behind the gas station to escape ("The Arrogant Suspect" from *The Fourth Decade* volume 2 – maryferrell.org).

1:26- Police Transcripts

Sgt. C.B. Owens- One of the men here at the service station that saw him seems to think he is in this block, 400 block East Jefferson behind his service station, give me some more squads over here.

The question arises from the above dispatch – Why didn't Sgt. Owens search the parking lot? Was there anyone there or not? Why did everyone go to the church instead of the parking lot?

1:26 – According to the FBI's calculations Oswald would enter the Texas Theater at this time. CD 87- "Shooting of Officer Tippit, then walked to Texas Theater at 231 W. Jefferson .6 mile. TIME 10 minutes."

CE 2593- "Mileage from 404 East Tenth Street to the Texas Theater, 231 West Jefferson, is .7 miles. The following route was used for measurement: West on 10th Street to Patton, south on Patton to Jefferson, west on Jefferson to the Texas Theatre, 231 West Jefferson. The above measurements were made by using the odometer in a 1964 Plymouth, Secret Service car number 466."

1:26-1:30 (estimated) – Truly tells officers that Oswald is missing from the TSBD. This happens after the rifle is found by Weitzman, according the Dallas PD Nov. 22 report (texashistory.unt.edu).

1:28 – Jack Ruby is seen at Parkland Hospital by an acquaintance of his named Seth Kantor (HSCA V. 9).

1:30 – Bugliosi places Truly's "roll call" of TSBD employees at this time. Truly tells Deputy Chief Lumpkin that Oswald is missing, and the two of them tell Captain Fritz. Fritz receives Oswald's description "23 years old, five foot nine, about a hundred and fifty pounds."

1:30 – According to George Applin, the lights in the theater go on at this time. Two police officers walk down the two aisles of the theater. Applin gets up from his seat and walks to the back of the theater. He sees officers "shake down" two men sitting near the front of the theater, and then he sees the Oswald scuffle. Oswald pulls out a gun and points it at the officer's head. Oswald pulls the trigger but the gun does not go off. (From Applin's December 16 testimony.)

Time Unknown -(WC V. 7) According to Warren Commission testimony, Johnny Brewer, 22, manager of Hardy's Downtown Shoe Store at 213 West Jefferson, has heard the news of Kennedy's assassination on the radio. He hears police cars going up Jefferson and sees a man go into the lobby of the shoe store. "He was a little man, about 5'9", and weighed about 150 pounds is all...And had brown hair. He had a brown sports shirt on. His shirt tail was out...Light complexioned." The man walks toward the Texas Theater. Brewer goes onto the street and watches him enter the theater. "He just looked funny to me. Well, in the first place, I had seen him some place before. I think he had been in my store before. And when you wait on somebody, you recognize them, and he just seemed funny. His hair was sort of messed up and he looked like he'd been running, and he looked scared, and he looked funny." The man walks into the theater. Brewer asks Mrs. Julia Postal if she had sold a ticket to the man with the brown shirt and she says no, she hasn't. She'd been listening to the radio as well. Brewer walks inside and asks Butch Burroughs, who works concessions, if he's seen a man with a brown shirt, and Burroughs says that he hasn't. Brewer asks to check all the exits, because the man looked suspicious.

Brewer and Burroughs check the exits and search the theater but do not find the man with the brown shirt. There are about 15 or 20 people in the theater. They go back out front to tell Julia Postal that they cannot find him, and she calls the police. Butch goes to the front exit and Brewer goes to the stage to guard the back exit. They wait for the police to arrive. The police turn on the house lights and Brewer sees the man, six or seven rows from the back, in the middle of the aisle. Brewer tells the police that there is a man in the theater he is suspicious of, and he points him out. An officer approaches Oswald. There is a scuffle and Oswald hits Officer MacDonald. Oswald says, "I am not resisting arrest," twice, as the police handcuff him and take him out of the theater. Brewer does not remember what time the officers entered the theater.

According to her Warren Commission testimony, Julia Postal sees Oswald "duck into" the theater, but does nothing. She clearly does not believe him to be suspicious. When confronted by Brewer, she tells him Oswald did not pay for a ticket. Butch Burroughs, who did not see Oswald enter, testifies that Oswald probably went first to the balcony, very quickly.

Neither Julia Postal, Butch Burroughs, nor Johnny Brewer tell the Warren Commission what time Oswald entered the theater. Julia Postal testifies that 24 people bought tickets to the movie between 12:45 (when the box office opened) and 1:15.

1:30 – According to Johnny Brewer's Dallas County affidavit of December 6 (texashistory.unt.edu), Oswald is standing in front of the shoe store at this time. Oswald proceeds to walk toward the theater. Oswald seems nervous, and so Brewer thinks that this may be the man who shot the policeman. Exactly how he knew that a policeman had been shot is unknown. Oswald enters the theater and Brewer follows him. Julia Postal does not remember if Oswald has bought a ticket and Butch Burroughs has not seen Oswald at all. Brewer and Burroughs search the theater and does not find Oswald.

Note: It is essential to assess what Brewer knew, when he saw Oswald, and what his motives were. The radio ostensibly reported Tippit's death in the fourteen minutes following his murder at 1:16, but as yet no radio broadcasts proving this have been located; all commercial radio broadcasts available seem to be reporting Kennedy's death, updates on Connally's health, and live broadcasts from Dealey Plaza at this time. The police don't even receive a description of Tippit's killer until 1:23, and there is no evidence that the news of Tippit's murder is broadcast on any radio station before 2:00. Between 1:20 and 1:30, Brewer would have heard on the radio that the suspect was possibly still in the TSBD or its immediate vicinity, and he also would have heard that several suspects had been arrested already.

So Brewer's motivation for following Oswald remains unclear. As Manchester says, it would not be until forty minutes after Tippit's shooting at 1:15 "that anyone suspected the significance of the officer's death" –

hence, not until Oswald's arrest would the world suspect that the two murders were linked. In a 1996 interview with Ian Griggs in The Dealey Plaza Echo (Vol. 1 Issue 3) Brewer stated that he knew he heard about Kennedy's arrest on the radio, but forgets which station — it may have been KLIF. He recalls hearing something about a shooting in the Oak Cliff area, but remembers few details. He heard a brief description of a shooter, and noticed police sirens and saw police cars driving past the shop. There was no connection between the Oak Cliff shooting and the President's shooting. He noticed Oswald walk down Jefferson, from Zangs, the direction of Tippit's shooting. As Bishop says, "It seemed like a lot of trouble for one ninety-cent gate crasher, but Brewer was going to follow his lead all the way." As we see, even lone nut theorists have trouble explaining Brewer's reaction to Oswald entering the theater.

1:30 – Julia Postal, in her affidavit of December 4, places Oswald's entry at 1:30 or a little later. She describes listening to KLIF and hearing that the President has been shot – she does not mention hearing about Tippit's murder. She sees Oswald duck inside the theater as the police drive by. Strangely, she does not react to Oswald's failure to buy a ticket. Brewer appears and asks if that man had bought a ticket, and Postal strangely replies "What man?" Brewer specifies, the man who just entered the theater. Postal then recalls that the man did not buy a ticket. Brewer asks if he can go search the theater, which he does. Brewer searches the theater with Burroughs and returns, telling Postal that the man is nowhere to be found. Postal urges the two to check the theater again, just to be sure. They do so.

When they return, Postal tells Brewer and Burroughs to guard the exits and make sure no one leaves. She says she is going to call the police, which she does. She tells the female operator that she wants to talk to a police officer. When she is connected to an officer, she tells him that there's a man in the theater who is hiding from the police, but the man can't be found. When asked what makes her think he is still in the theater, Postal replies that it might be women's intuition, but she just knows he's in there. The officer asks Postal if the man fits the description of the suspect of the President's murder, and Postal replies that she hasn't heard the description of the President's killer. Postal then describes Oswald (whom she only saw very briefly, out of the corner of her eye, as she was watching the police cars drive by). The officer says he will send somebody out to the theater. Postal then ends the phone call and calls the projectionist to ask if he sees the suspect in the theater. The projectionist says no, and asks if he should stop the movie. Postal tells him not to, and hangs up. The police show up about one or two minutes later, and they emerge about ten minutes after that with Oswald. (It is notable that women's intuition sent 16 officers racing to the Texas Theater, and convinced half of them that the suspect was in the balcony.)

Note: Postal's testimony lines up roughly with Brewer's timing, below, for a 1:30 entrance for Oswald. It may be possible for the theater search and her call to the police to take place before 1:45. But she claims the police were in the theater for about ten minutes before they emerged with Oswald. If the dispatcher's report went out right before 1:46 (according to the transcript), police wouldn't enter at the building until at least one minute later. Bugliosi has the police arriving at 1:48, which *seems reasonable when we look at the transcript. But this reduces the arrival of 16 officers, the theater search, the scuffle, the arrest, the arrival of the press and 200 onlookers, and the placement of Oswald in the car at 1:51, to three minutes. This affidavit also does not tell us why the dispatcher thought the suspect was in the balcony.*

1:31-(CD 728 Police Transcripts)

87 – A white station wagon believed to be PE 3435, unknown make and model, late model, occupied by 2 W/M left this fellow's station going east on Davis and believed to have a shotgun or rifle in the backseat.

111- They say he is running West in the alley between Jefferson and 10th.

Dispatcher – West in the alley between Jefferson and 10th.

Note: According to Julia Postal and Johnny Brewer, Oswald entered the theater at this time, when suspects on the scene told officers that the Tippit shooter was still running west in the alley after dropping his white jacket and hiding behind the service station on Jefferson.

44 – That was where on 10th street? What address?

Unknown – 44, that was 501 E. 10th street. Running west from that location, a white male, 30, 5'8", black hair, white jacket, black trousers, white shirt. Had either rifle or shotgun in back seat, license on car, prefix PE – no other information.

41 – Was suspect on foot or in car?

Unknown – On foot at that time.

1:32 – Police Transcripts

44- Report from City radio just now that jacket has been found at scene. Probably won't have a jacket on.

1:33- Kennedy's death is announced by White House Assistant Press Secretary Malcolm Kilduff at Parkland (Manchester).

1:33 – According to McBride, news of Kennedy's death and the murder of a policeman in Oak Cliff are   both broadcast for the first time on a local Dallas radio station. Evidence is not provided.

Police Transcripts

1:33 - 111 (Pollard) – They say he is running west in the alley between Jefferson and 10th.

Unknown- Clothing the description on that suspect.

Dispatcher – White male, 30, 5'8", very slender build, black hair, a white jacket, white shirt and black slacks, 1:33.

223- (Patrolman C.T. Walker) – He is in the library, Jefferson East 500 block, Marsalis and Jefferson.

221 (Summers)- Might can give you some additional information. I got eye-ball witness to the getaway man; that suspect in this shooting. He is a white male, 27, 5'11", 165, black wavy hair, fair complected, wearing light gray Eisenhower-type jacket, dark trousers and a white shirt and but last seen running on the north side of the street from Patton on Jefferson; on East Jefferson, and was apparently armed with a .32, dark finish, automatic pistol which he had in his right hand."

Dispatcher- For your information, 221, they have the suspect cornered in the library Marsalis and Jefferson.

Summers – 104. This man can positively identify him if they need him.

Dispatcher – Well, they have the man under arrest now.

Owens- It was the wrong man.

Summers – I'm in front of 404 West – East 10th right now. I got two witnesses – the one that talked to the officer and one that observed the man.

550 (Patrolman Westbrook) – We got a witness that saw him go up North Jefferson and he shed his jacket – let's check that vicinity, towards Tyler.

Sgt Hill- The shell at the scene indicates that the suspect is armed with an automatic .38 rather than a pistol.

Note: Tyler Street runs north and south and intersects Jefferson 7/10 of a mile west of the Texas Theater. The officer seems to imply that the suspect was seen traveling north of Jefferson and west of the theater. Oswald was supposedly entering the theater at this time.

1:33 –(CD 728)

23 – Zangs and Clarendon.

… Unknown – What was the description on that suspect.

Dispatcher – W/M/30/ 5-8", very slender build, black hair, a white jacket, white shirt and dark slacks, 1:33.

19 – 19.

Dispatcher – 19.

19 - Do you know what kind of a call he was on?

Dispatcher – What kind of what?

19 - Was he on a call or anything?

Dispatcher – No.

19- 10-4.

Dispatcher – Do you have any information for us, 19?

19 – No, we are shaking down these old houses in the 400 block East Jefferson right now.

95 – 95.

Dispatcher – Go ahead.

95 – Send me a squad over here 10th and Crawford to check out this church basement.

Dispatcher – Any squad 10th and Crawford.

63- 63 is enroute.

1:34

35- In area on 10th street.

Dallas 1?

44 – Zangs and Davis.

Dallas 1.

Dallas 1.

For the attention of all officers, this is an anonymous tip only. A green '57 Ford, bearing Texas license DT4857 with white male as occupant. If located, acknowledge. Advise this department.

Note: Interestingly, no witnesses in the area around Patton and Jefferson in the minutes following Tippit's shooting have connected the Tippit shooter with someone who entered the Texas Theater. No one saw Oswald running down West Jefferson. At 1:34, the police are still searching the area immediately surrounding Tippit's murder, assuming the shooter is hiding there, even though the shooter was seen running west on Jefferson, or in the alley between 10th and Jefferson. It is notable that the police did not go west on Jefferson in their search. Zang and Davis is several blocks northwest of the area. Johnny Brewer, who says he saw Oswald enter at around 1:30, of course did not see Oswald leaving the scene of the Tippit shooting. Notice below, the police are intensively searching the library at Marsalis and Jefferson, two blocks east of the Tippit shooting, from 1:35- 1:38, while Oswald has apparently been in the theater for several minutes. Why the police did not follow the killer west, where he was last seen running, is a mystery.

1:30-1:35 – Scoggins and his passenger (Callaway, who is carrying Tippit's gun) pass a police car. The passenger stops the car and talks with the officers. He takes the passenger back to the scene of the crime, and the passenger gives the gun to the police. This is when Scoggins realizes his passenger is not a police officer. The police continue questioning people at the scene, but not Scoggins.

Scoggins describes Tippit's shooter as a "medium height fellow with, kind of a slender look, and approximately, I said, 25, 26 years old." His description goes on: medium brown or dark hair, white skin, light complected, not real brown, slender but not real slender, not wearing glasses. The next day, the 23rd, Scoggins is picked up by the police down at the cab stand shortly after lunch and taken to the police station. That morning he has seen a picture of Oswald in the morning newspaper shown to him by one of the other cab drivers. *(By this time Oswald's picture, the news of his arrest, and the insinuation of his guilt were widely spread throughout the media. It would've been hard not to identify him as the killer. See CE 2142-2146 for the TV reel transcripts from the 22nd and 23rd in which Chief Curry repeatedly discusses the evidence against Oswald, calling him the "prime suspect.")* Scoggins, unsurprisingly, tells the WC that he believed Oswald was the same man he saw running away from the Tippit shooting. Scoggins is shown a lineup of four people, including Oswald. He identifies Oswald as the suspect, another man who looks similar to the suspect, and two others who are shorter. Oswald is wearing different clothes than the man Scoggins has seen: "He had on a different shirt, and he didn't have a jacket on. He had on kind of a polo shirt."

After the lineup a man who Scoggins thinks is either FBI or Secret Service shows Scoggins his credentials and asks Scoggins to identify the shooter from a stack of 4 or 5 photos. Scoggins narrows the photos down to two that resemble the suspect. "I told him one of these two pictures is him, out of this group he showed me, and the one that was actually him looked like an older man to me. Of course, I am not too much on identifying pictures. It wasn't a full shot of him, you know, and then he told me the other one was Oswald."

1:35 – Manchester has Oswald running past the Bethel Temple, but does not say where it is. This is 20 minutes after the Tippit shooting. The Texas Theater is 6/10 of a mile from the Tippit site, yet Oswald is still running there. Did he stop somewhere? Did he take a circuitous route? We do not know.

1:35 - Police transcript

221 - Might can give you some additional information. I got an eye-ball witness to the get-away man. That suspect in this shooting is a white male, twenty-seven, five feet eleven, a hundred sixty-five, black wavy hair, fair complected, wearing a light grey Eisenhower-type jacket, dark trousers and a white shirt, and (. . . ?). Last seen running on the north side of the street from Patton, on Jefferson, on East Jefferson. And he was apparently armed with a 32 dark-finish automatic pistol which he had in his right hand.

1:35 (estimated) – KRLD reports that a 24 or 25-year-old suspect has been arrested and a 5-story building surrounded in downtown Dallas. The report came from Dan Rather 15 minutes ago and nothing more has been heard since then.

1:35 – Lyndon Johnson and his party board Air Force One; as Manchester says, at this time "it was logical to suppose that the great crime had been committed by a great criminal, backed, perhaps, by a great criminal nation."

1:36 – According to Bugliosi, Johnny Brewer first witnesses Oswald step into the lobby of Hardy's Shoe Store on Jefferson. Brewer's suspicions arise from the fact that Oswald seems to be avoiding the police driving west on Jefferson (when most police were in fact searching the library .7 miles away at this time), and Oswald has a disheveled appearance. Bugliosi believes Brewer had heard on the radio that a cop had been shot "less than three quarters of a mile away" by this time. This is doubtful (see note below, at 1:45). Bugliosi provides the nine-minute window of 1:36 to 1:45 for Brewer to go to the theater, talk to Julia Postal, search the theater with Butch Burroughs, and tell Postal to call the police.

1:37 (CD 728)

Unknown -Any units Marsallis and Jefferson. Go to library. 1:37 PM.

Note: Remember that Oswald was supposedly trying to avoid the police when he entered the theater anywhere from 1:30 to 1:40, when police were searching the church and the library, over a half a mile east, during these ten minutes. There is no indication from transcripts that police were traveling west on Jefferson at the Texas Theater this time. They certainly were not searching the area around the theater, and no police stopped Oswald as he walked down Jefferson toward the theater, though he ostensibly resembled the Tippit suspect. The Oswald who shot Tippit, muttered "Poor dumb cop," threatened to kill Helen Markham and sauntered away from the site, who according to Markham "Wasn't in no hurry or anything," is hard to reconcile with the nervous wreck who hid from police in Johnny Brewer's lobby before racing into the theater – especially when police were not searching the area.

1:40 (CD 677) – Kennedy's casket arrives at Parkland Hospital. This casket has been ordered by SA Hill at the request of Kenneth O'Donnell. The casket is taken into the emergency room, and Kennedy's body is placed into the casket.

1:40 (CD 677) – President and Mrs. Johnson arrive at Love Field and board Air Force One. The President and Mrs. Johnson are joined in the stateroom by Congressmen Thornberry, Brooks, and Thomas. ASAIC Youngblood remains with the President. The President summons the Attorney General to discuss legal aspects of taking the oath. He summons Federal Judge Sarah Hughes to the plane. Johnson asks to be informed of the location of Mrs. Kennedy and the body of the President, and to be informed when they arrive at the plane.

1:40 – Police Transcripts

Sgt. Gerald Hill - A witness reports that he was last seen in the Abundant Life Temple about the 400 block. We are fixing to go in and shake it down.

Dispatcher – Is that the one that was involved in the shooting of the officer?

Hill – Yes.

Dispatcher – They already have him.

1:40 – A Dallas Police Department document lists this as the time for Oswald's arrest ("List of Arresting Officers and Times of Arrest, texashistory.unt.edu). Officers present at the Texas Theater during the arrest: Baggett, Barrett, Bentley, Buhk, Carroll, Cunningham, Hawkins, Hill, Hutson, Lyons, McDonald, Stringer, Taylor, Toney, Walker, and Westbrook.

M.N. McDonald also provides 1:40 as the time of Oswald's arrest in his "Arrest Report of Investigative

Prisoner" (texashistory.unt.edu). He writes: "This man shot and killed President John F. Kennedy and Police Officer J.D. Tippit. He also shot and wounded Governor John Connally."

1:40 – Detective Bentley, at City Hall, receives information about the Tippit shooting and goes to 10th and Patton with Captain Doughty and Sgt. Barnes. They arrive at the Tippit site. They are there for five minutes when they hear that the suspect is in the Texas Theater. Bentley goes to the theater with Captain Talbert. When he arrives, Bentley is told by Det. Toney that the suspect is in the balcony. Bentley goes to the balcony and tells the projectionist to turn on the houselights. Bentley searches the balcony and does not find Oswald, then goes to the first floor and witnesses the scuffle. Bentley's timing places the scuffle and arrest quite close to 2:00 (Bentley's letter to Chief Curry, texashistory.unt.edu).

1:40 – CE 1120 provides this time for Oswald's arrival at the Texas Theater.

CE 1987- "The distance from the location in the 400 block of East 10th street to the Texas Theater, 231 West Jefferson, a distance of 6/10 of a mile, was walked at a brisk pace by SA Barret in 10 minutes." As mentioned above, Oswald should have run into the theater at 1:26, if he was heading straight down Jefferson as we are told he was. Why didn't the Warren Commission move the entry time to 1:25-1:30? Because that provides a large window, almost twenty minutes, when Oswald was in the theater and no one called the police. As it is, we have an uncomfortably large window, 1:16-1:40, when Oswald's whereabouts are unaccounted for (assuming he killed Tippit – if he didn't kill Tippit, the window is 1:03-1:40).

One possibility is that Oswald entered the movie theater at an improbably early time, far too early for him to have killed Tippit, and the police, knowing somehow that he was going to be there, and that he was to be the suspect in both killings, had to invent a reason to go arrest him there. That raises the problem of Brewer, Burroughs and Postal – what part did they really play in the arrest of Oswald? Only Brewer claimed to have seen Oswald clearly, and he alone was the instigator of the entire arrest of Oswald at the theater. Perhaps he was the only witness who agreed to work with the police in the arrest. Brewer would have to have known ahead of time that Oswald was going into the theater, so that he could go direct Postal and Burroughs to help him search the theater and call the police. This is not impossible – it would only take one person to go and inform Brewer ahead of time what his role was to be. He did take an unusually active role, compared to Postal and Burroughs, who should've been more certain than they were of Oswald's suspicious behavior, being employees in the theater.

1:40- Manchester also has Oswald entering the theater at this time, 25 minutes after the Tippit shooting. Why it took Oswald 25 minutes to run 6/10 of a mile is not addressed by Manchester.

According to the Warren Report, Brewer sees Oswald enter the theater, tells Julia Postal that he did not buy a ticket (a fact that she should've known, since she was the cashier) and tells Postal to call the police. This all occurs shortly after 1:40.

The following transmission appears to occur at 1:40 (CD 728):

All units at Marsallis and Jefferson disregard. This is wrong suspect. 1:40 PM.

All units standby unless you have emergency traffic. 1:40 PM.

For attention of all units: THE PRESIDENT IS DEAD.

35 -Out at Texas Theater on West Jefferson.

44 – Did you advise you were clear? What you got at the Texas Theater?

35 – They got a suspect hiding in the balcony at the Texas Theater on West Jefferson. I'll be out.

44 – I'll be en route.

1:43 – Dispatcher – 87 (Nelson), was that a Pontiac or a Falcon?

Nelson- He didn't say what kind of car it would be. He said it was a white car with a luggage rack on top. He wasn't sure of the model, talked like it was a big car, though.

Sgt. H.H. Stringer – The jacket that suspect was wearing over here on Jefferson bears a label tag with the letter B 9738. See if there is any way you can check the laundry tag.

Note: According to CD 868, Hoover's letter to J. Lee Rankin, the FBI found that the jacket's "laundry mark and/or cleaning tag was not identified as originating from any cleaning or laundry establishment in the

Greater Dallas, Texas, area." Hoover's letter identifies the laundry mark as 30 030, however – not B9738.

1:44

Nelson – What was the last location anybody had on the location of the suspect in Oak Cliff?

Dispatcher -Running north on Patton. *(Note- This is in the opposite direction of the theater and it must be the dispatcher's mistake, since all witnesses, and police on the scene, said Tippit's shooter ran south on Patton and West on Jefferson.)*

1:44- Bugliosi has Johnny Brewer and Butch Brewer emerging from the theater at this time, to tell Julia Postal that they have not seen the suspect but he is probably still inside.

1:45- Police Transcripts

Dispatcher- We have information that suspect just went in the Texas Theater on West Jefferson.

Patrolman Arglin - 10-4.

Dispatcher - He's supposed to be hiding in the balcony.

Arglin – 10-4.

85 – Ptm. Walker – 85 out that way.

(Note - Neither Julia Postal, Johnny Brewer nor Butch Burroughs saw Oswald go into the balcony. This furthers the suspicion that the police had information that is not present in the transcripts and did not come from any known witness.)

J. Edgar Hoover, from his conversation with Lyndon Johnson on 11/29: "Then he walked about another two blocks and went to the theater and the woman at the theater window, selling the tickets...she was so suspicious...the way he was acting...she said he was carrying a gun...he had a revolver at that time...with which he had killed the police officer...he went into the theater and she notified the police and the police and our man down there went in there and located this particular man. They had quite a struggle with him...he fought like a regular lion...and he had to be subdued, of course, and was then brought out and, of course, taken to police headquarters...but, he apparently had come down the five flights of steps - stairway- from the fifth floor...so far as we've found out the elevator was not used...although he could have used it...but nobody remembers whether it was or whether it wasn't."

It should be clear how inaccurate Hoover's characterization is. This is all part of much larger campaign which originated at the FBI, to posthumously portray Oswald as crazed and dangerous, when there is little evidence to support this.

Unsurprisingly, *Life* does not give a time for the Texas Theater entrance. According to Johnny Brewer, Oswald is breathing heavily and his shirt is untucked when he stops in front of the shoe store. Oswald *dashes* a half block to the theater. According to *Life*, neither the cashier nor the usher see him enter. There is no word on when the movie has started.

CD 87 – "Total elapsed time from assassination of President Kennedy to entering of Texas Theater 49:25 minutes." (Note- This would put Oswald in the theater at around 1:19, when he had just left the Tippit scene).

Note: Google Maps lists the distance from 400 E. 10th Street, the location of the Tippit murder, to 231 West Jefferson, the location of the Texas Theater, as 0.6 miles, with a walking time of 13 minutes. If Oswald left the Tippit shooting at 1:16, this would put Oswald in the theater, assuming he went straight there without stopping (walking on Jefferson the whole way), at 1:29. Brewer gave 1:30 as the time for Oswald's entry in only one case, his Dallas County affidavit of December 6 (see 1:30 entry above). Why the theater entrance was changed to 1:40 is a mystery. Apparently during his run to the theater, Oswald stopped and refilled his .38 Smith and Wesson, which had bullets in all six chambers when he was arrested. (According to J.D. Tippit's autopsy, he was shot four times - texashistory.unt.edu). Questions arise: If this was Oswald, was he planning on going to the theater? If not, where was he heading and why did he go into the theater? Was he running the whole way, or was he walking? Why didn't he buy a ticket, since it would clearly arouse suspicion to enter without paying? Why did he reload his gun?

As we see below, by 1:45 the dispatcher reports that the suspect has entered the Texas Theater, and by 1:51 the suspect is in a police car, en route to City Hall. This gives Brewer, Burroughs and Postal, and the dispatcher at the most, 14 minutes for the following: to see Oswald enter; decide he is the killer of Tippit (when only Brewer, who recognized Oswald as a former customer in his shoe store, claims to have seen Oswald clearly); for Burroughs (who never saw Oswald enter) to search the theater with Brewer for ten to fifteen minutes without seeing Oswald; for Julia Postal (who saw Oswald for only an instant, and couldn't remember whether he'd bought a ticket or not) to call the police, convincing the dispatcher that the Tippit murder suspect is in the theater, when the police only had a vague description of Tippit's killer and Brewer himself probably hadn't heard a description of him; and then for the dispatcher to announce this information. According to the police dispatches, by 1:47 *five squads* were covering the back exit of the theater.

The official Warren Commission timeline has Oswald entering at 1:40, ten minutes later than Brewer's testimony. This ten minute discrepancy is not only factually problematic, but a 1:40 arrival gives an impossibly short period of time, just five minutes, for the above scenario to happen. Why would the Commission push back the entry time?

Many radio broadcasts from November 22 incorrectly state that a Secret Service Agent was killed in the attack, and some broadcasters later assume this to be a mistaken description of Tippit. If anything, Brewer would have heard that Kennedy, Connally, and a Secret Service Agent were shot in an assassination attempt downtown, and that the suspect was still in the Texas School Book Depository or the immediate vicinity of Dealey Plaza. Some networks broadcast the *5'10", 165 pounds, 30 years old* description, but it is not common to hear on the broadcasts. According to the Dallas Police "Report on Events Following the President's Murder," it wasn't until after 1:25 that Roy Truly even told police that Oswald was missing from the building (texashistory.unt.edu). So Brewer would have little reason to believe the President's killer was at large and roaming in his neighborhood. And he could not have heard on the radio in the 12-14 minutes following Tippit's murder that a policeman in Oak Cliff had been killed by a white, black haired, 5'8," 150 pound man fleeing west on Jefferson, who also resembled the President's killer.

So: What did Brewer really think and do, and when? And how did the police decide that the man described by Julia Postal was Tippit's killer, and most importantly, *when did Oswald enter the theater?*

As we will see, there is little clarity in the many testimonies and reports regarding the timeline. The Warren Commission, as evidenced below, is almost pathologically reluctant to ask witnesses what time any event occurred. This is regardless of who is being interviewed or who is asking the questions.

What is obvious is this: There is an effort, whose motives are not quite clear, to obscure the timing of Oswald's entry into the theater. Since not a single witness was ever asked by the Commission when he entered, it can be assumed that the Commission knew that these witnesses would be providing wildly inconsistent or problematic entry times, possibly in conflict with the Tippit shooting. There is no other explanation of the reluctance to establish when Oswald entered the theater.

1:40-1:45 (WC 3)– Officer McDonald, after hearing that the suspect has gone into the Texas Theater, drives there to see that several police cars are already at the scene. He enters through the rear, where two or three officers are already guarding the exit. He encounters a man inside wearing a suit, who tells him that the suspect is not in the balcony but is sitting downstairs in the orchestra seats, in the back of the theater, alone. The man with the suit (Johnny Brewer) points out the suspect to McDonald. McDonald walks up the aisle to two men who are sitting together and asks them to stand up. He searches them for weapons. He looks back at the man who has been pointed out to him (Oswald). Oswald is still sitting in his seat, not moving. Notably, Oswald never tries to flee when the police enter the building. McDonald states that he did not approach Oswald immediately because he did not want to overlook anybody or anything. McDonald walks toward Oswald at a normal gait, not looking directly at him but keeping his eye on him. McDonald walks slowly past Oswald, then turns suddenly and tells him to get on his feet. A struggle ensues, with Oswald knocking McDonald's hat off and attempting to shoot him with the .38 Smith and Wesson. After a struggle of unknown duration, involving several officers, Oswald is handcuffed. McDonald gives Oswald's gun to Detective Bob Carroll.

According to Joesten, the FBI reported that the firing pin on Oswald's gun was so damaged as to be unusable. Joesten questions how and why Oswald had done this on his flight to the theater. Joesten also questions the placement of Oswald's gun - how did he take it out of his pocket and point it at McDonald's head (according to a press conference with Wade) while engaged in a scuffle with McDonald?

From "Leftist Accused," NY Times Nov. 22: "Then another call came to police headquarters from Julia Postal, cashier of the Texas Theater at 231 West Jefferson Boulevard, six blocks from the scene of the policeman's slaying. She said an usher had told her that a man who had just entered the theater was acting peculiarly. The investigating officers were dispatched to the theater. They began checking patrons, starting at the front of the house."

1:45 – Police enter the Texas Theater, according to George Applin's Nov. 22 affidavit (texashistory.unt.edu). His description of the scuffle and arrest is similar to official police accounts.

1:45 PM (CE 343)– According to the *Dallas Morning News* of November 28, 1963, Oswald enters the theater at 1:45. This reflects a strange trend among in some reports to push back the entry and subsequent arrest to a fifteen minute time frame starting at 1:45. This of course raises the question of what Oswald was doing for 30 minutes after he killed Tippit. "About 1:45 p.m., Julia Postal, cashier at the Texas Theater at 231 West Jefferson, saw a hurrying stranger push past her into the theater. To this day, she can't remember if he paid or not...Five minutes or more had elapsed before Johnny Brewer, manager of a shoe store a few doors away, ran in. Mrs. Postal said he thought he had seen 'someone running from the police' duck into the theater. The cashier immediately called the police – who had just sped en masse to a false alarm at the Dallas Library...the police sirens wailed again...Police went in the Texas Theater to the machine gun clatter of a movie called 'War is Hell.' They found their man – hiding in a middle-section seat."

From CD 87, report by Special Agent Roger Warner (December 6, 1963): "Brewer observed Oswald walking west on Jefferson in the 200 block of Jefferson in a suspicious manner. He followed Oswald until Oswald entered the Texas Theater...

"Miss Postal stated that she was in the cashier's booth at the Texas Theater, listening to broadcasts relative to the assassination of President Kennedy...Miss Postal stated that she heard police sirens and stepped out of the cashier's booth to the sidewalk. At this time, she stated, she observed Oswald out of the corner of her eye standing near the entrance to the theater. Miss Postal stated she watched the street for a few seconds and then returned to the cashier's booth. She feels that she did see Oswald enter the theater but she cannot be sure of this fact. When she returned to the booth, Johnny Brewer asked if she sold Oswald a ticket. Miss Postal stated that she had not. Miss Postal observed Brewer walk into the theater. Brewer stated that he was going to look for Oswald. Brewer returned later and told Postal that he had not been able to locate the man and asked her to call the police, which she did. Brewer then returned into the theater and with Usher Warren Burrs stood at the exit doors. Miss Postal stated that even though she had just a quick glance at Oswald, she was quite sure he was not carrying a gun at the time he entered the theater. Miss Postal stated that she had not observed the actual arrest inside the theater and could only report that when Oswald was brought out of the theater by police officers, a crowd had gathered and were yelling, 'Kill him. Kill him.'...

"At a few minutes to 2:00 P.M., on November 22, 1963, police officers received a call to proceed to the Texas Theater as the suspect in the murder of Officer Tippit was reported as being in that theater. Officers converged on the theater where they were met by Mr. Warren Burrs and Mr. Brewer. The officers were informed that the suspect was in the balcony and several officers searched the balcony with negative results. The lights of the theater were turned on just after the officers arrived at the theater." Officer McDonald approaches Oswald and a struggle ensues. McDonald is joined by several other officers. Oswald pulls out a .36 caliber pistol and in the struggle the pistol action snaps as the hammer falls. However, a shell is not discharged. At the station, Patrolman McDonald examines the pistol and finds in the chamber 6 full rounds with one round dented, which indicates it had misfired.

"The exact time of arrest has not been ascertained at this time, however, all officers agree that it was approximately 2:00 P.M."

This report also does not mention the time that Oswald entered the theater.

Unknown Time – (WC V.7) According to his Warren Commission testimony, Dallas Police Sergeant Gerald Hill enters the Texas Theater with two or three other officers and they go up into the balcony. At this time the movie is still playing. He yells to a theater employee to turn on the theater lights. There are six people on the balcony. The officers check them out, and none of them fit the profile of Tippit's shooter. He goes out onto the fire escape and sees Officer C.E. Talbert on the ground. They converse, and Talbert agrees to start up the fire escape to search on the roof. He searches the balcony again, and heads downstairs when he hears a shout from the first floor to the effect of "I've got him." He runs down the right aisle toward a group of officers who are struggling with a white male. Someone tells Hill "Look out, he's got a gun." After a struggle of unknown duration, Hill says that "We finally got the man subdued..." Hill asks Hawkins for some handcuffs, which are produced, and Oswald is handcuffed. An FBI agent named Bob Barnett, whom Hill was not familiar with at the time, enters the theater from the rear exits. Captain Westbrook instructs the officers to get the suspect out of the theater as soon as they can. As the officers take Oswald into the lobby they are greeted by a large crowd of people, including a man "shooting movies" from channel 8 news. A large crowd has gathered outside, with people shouting "'That is him. We ought to kill him. String him up. Hang him,' etc. and so on." Hill estimates the crowd to number about 200.

The police have parted the crowd to make way for the officers to bring Oswald out. Hill takes Oswald to the police car. Hill is in the front middle, with K.E. Lyons in the right front. In the back are, from left to right, Bentley, Oswald, and Walker. Bob Carroll gets in the driver's seat, with Hill in the middle of the front, and hands a pistol to Hill, telling him that this was the gun taken from the suspect in the theater. It is a .38 Smith and Wesson, with a 2" barrel that contains six shells. There are six live rounds in the chambers of the gun, and one of the rounds has an indention caused by the hammer. The car begins its trip to City Hall. Within seconds of the car starting, Hill radios to the dispatcher that they have the suspect and are heading to the station. By this time it is 1:51.

An alternative timeline suggests itself. This is of course entirely speculative, but seems to make more sense than the official timeline: 1:25 – Brewer, who has been told to watch out for Oswald, finally notices him walk down the street and enter the theater. For whatever reason, Postal and Burroughs later claim to have little or no awareness of Oswald's presence at the theater. Oswald has walked straight to the theater from his rooming house on Beckley. (Google Maps gives a 21 minute walking time from the rooming house to the Texas Theater, assuming he walked south on Beckley and turned right on Jefferson. If Oswald left the rooming house on foot at 1:04, 1:25 is a suitable time for his arrival at the theater.) By this time the search for Tippit's killer has just begun, and Oswald is not picked up as a suspect as he walks down Jefferson to enter the theater. 1:26 – Brewer enters the theater and speaks to Julia Postal, attempting to rile her up, because he knows he has to call the police to come pick up this man and he will need other witnesses. She has not noticed anyone strange enter the theater, but agrees to let Brewer search it. Brewer speaks to Butch Burroughs, operating the concessions counter, who also did not see anyone strange enter. This does not mean that Burroughs or Postal did not see Oswald enter – it just means no one suspicious, matching Brewer's description, entered. 1:27 – Brewer and Burroughs begin searching the theater. Brewer, who has seen Oswald at his store before, and has been told by the police to keep an eye out for him, is ostensibly searching for him, but in reality is making sure Oswald is in fact there before he tells Julia Postal to call the police. The police, who need a reason to go to the theater in the first place, must rely on a citizen who has seen Oswald behaving strangely, and Brewer is the only person who claims to have seen Oswald in this condition. Oswald, who may or may not notice that two men are searching the theater, does not flee at this time. He is clearly not at the theater to hide. Someone in hiding would be much more aware that the theater is being searched, and would probably leave the theater at that time. 1:40-1:43 – Brewer goes to Julia Postal in the cashier's office and tells her that the suspect is probably still in the theater and she should call the police. Postal, who barely remembered seeing Oswald, gives a vague description of him to the police, and probably does not tell them that he is in the balcony since no one has seen him go up there. Brewer goes to the back of the theater to make sure Oswald does not escape before police get there; he has been told to keep his eye on the suspect.

The fact that Oswald never tries to escape shows that he is not expecting to be arrested, and his behavior afterward indicates that he is completely shocked that the police have arrested him. Lone nut theorists like to use this as further proof of his insanity. 1:45- Dispatcher Murray Jackson (who has heard from someone other than Julia Postal that Oswald will be in the balcony) radios that a suspect has gone into the Texas Theater and is hiding in the balcony. In the next six minutes, the police enter the theater, a scuffle ensues, the press arrives to take photos of Oswald's arrest, a crowd of 200 assembles, and Oswald is placed in the police car. This suggests that the police knew before 1:45 that Oswald was in the theater, and were there even before 1:45. 1:51 – Oswald is on his way to City Hall.

1:45-1:50 - According to CD 87 (Secret Service Report) p. 669, "Approximately 10 or 15 minutes after Brewer arrived at the theater and while he was standing at the exit near the screen, the lights were turned on and at this time Brewer saw Oswald sitting in the center section 5 or 6 rows down from the rear. He saw Oswald stand up when the lights went on, walk to the right aisle, and then return to the seat he had left. At about this time, Brewer heard people about his exit and he opened the door. Police entered and grabbed Brewer who then explained to the police that Oswald was still in the theater. Brewer and one of the officers went to the stage where Brewer pointed to Oswald and at about this time officers entered from the rear and Officer McDonald went in toward Oswald."

After a struggle, Oswald is taken out through the front of the theater and Brewer hears him say "I'm not resisting arrest."

From CE 2160- NBC TV Interview with Sgt. Gerald Hill, November 22, 1963:

Q- Sir, did he make any statement? Did he say anything other than "this is it?"

Hill- He did not admit to us when he was in custody any of the accusations either of shooting the officer or of any other crime that could have been committed. He started demanding that he be allowed to see a lawyer and he started talking about his rights – wouldn't even admit that he had pulled the trigger on the gun in the theater. Actually we didn't receive any information as to the contents of the crime from him for the entire trip to the station.

Q- What about the matching descriptions, Jerry?

Hill- Approximately two inches in height was the only discrepancy in the description of the man who killed Officer Tippit and the man who shot the President.

Q- What was the description of that man?

Hill – He was described as five six to five eight, slight build, brown hair, having on a jacket and white shirt and dark trousers. Actually the subject was about five ten and had discarded the jacket which we found in the Oak

Cliff area near a funeral home in the 400 block of East Jefferson, and at the time we arrested the subject his pistol was again fully loaded and we had a witness that said he saw the subject stop long enough to reload his pistol after shooting the officer.

Q- What did you find in the building?

Q- Near where the President was shot from?

Hill – In the building on the sixth floor we found an area that, near a window, had been partially blocked off by boxes of books, and also the three spent shells that had apparently been fired from a rifle. Also we found the remnants of what could have been a meal eaten by the suspect of a chicken dinner *(Note: once again, this places Bonnie Ray Williams in the sniper's nest at 12:20, when Oswald should have been there waiting for the motorcade)*. At that time I left the building and later, I understand, in the same general vicinity under some boxes the rifle that was used was found.

Q- The rifle that we saw in the office?

Q- What did the man say when you arrested him?

Hill- The man did not make any definite statement other than demanding to see a lawyer and demanding his rights, and when we arrested him he did not volunteer any information at all. The only way we found out his name at all was to remove his billfold and check it ourselves; he wouldn't even tell us what his name was.

Q- What does he – do you believe he is the same man who killed the police officer?

Hill- Having been in it from the very beginning, as far as the officer's death is concerned, I am convinced that he is the man that killed the officer. Now the tie-in on the rest of it will have to be established by someone else. As to whether the two situations are related, other circumstances that are taking place in another part of the investigation other than what I have been connected with will have to be proved to tie the two together...

Q- Has the suspect admitted to shooting the President?

Hill- Not to my knowledge, he hasn't.

Q- What was the name on the billfold?

Hill- Lee Oswald. O-S-W-A-L-D.

Q - At no point did he say anything like "I've got me a President"?

Hill- Not when he was in my custody. I never heard him make a statement of that type.

Q- Did you hear that statement from anybody?

Hill- I have heard it as a rumor that was said, but I can't verify it because it was not said in my presence.

Q- Are you convinced, sir, that there are three men involved?

Hill- No sir, I am convinced that the man we have is the man that shot the officer. As to the circumstances that happened prior to the shooting, we can only surmise that the officer stopped a car, on possibly a traffic violation or on information from a citizen, but we can't verify that, and also the only two people who can tell us why the officer stopped him is the officer and the man who shot him...

Q- Where did you get your information on the presidential assassin?

Hill- Sir, it was broadcast on the air. As to what officer actually first received the information as to who the assassin was, I couldn't tell you.

Q- Wasn't there a description called in by some unknown person?

Hill- Suspect now?

Q- As far as the suspect is concerned?

Hill- The suspect will be interrogated some more. At the same time all the loose ends will be tied together to the best of our ability and the crime lab and other agencies involved that can supply us with additional information on the suspect will all be in operation until we try to tie this thing up in a neat package.

Q- Jerry, are there any fingerprints on the rifle?

Hill- But, as to the exact time, I don't know. Bill, I don't know for sure. I couldn't say one way or another.

Q- Any idea at all?

Q- Where were the spent bullets in the room?

Hill- I did not pick them up.

Q- Does the crime lab...idea?

Hill- I have no idea.

1:46 – Police Transcripts

550 – Do you have any additional information on this Oak Cliff suspect?

492 (CID) – 492, out Texas Theater.

Dispatcher – They think he is at Texas Theater, 550/2.

1:47- Barnes – Notify our office to send us four slides and need additional metallic kit. Extra metallic kit. Bring to the 6th floor down here at Houston and Elm.

Dispatcher – Have some squad cover off the rear of theater fire escape.

Hawkins – There's about five squads back here with me now.

1:48

Dispatcher - ...en route to Texas Theater. Have someone cover off the rear of the theater at the fire escape.

1:48 – Bugliosi has the police arriving at the theater at this time. Brewer is confronted by police, who mistake him for the suspect.

1:48- Police Transcripts

Sgt. C.B. Owens: Captain Talbert and some squads are going to the Texas Theater. I remain here at the scene.

1:50- Dallas Police Detective John Toney claims that at this time he, Lt. Cunningham, and Detective Buhk are cruising Oak Cliff and hear from the dispatcher that the suspect of a police shooting is in the Texas Theater in the balcony. They head to the theater ("Report of John Toney to Chief Curry," Dec. 3, texashistory.unt.edu).

1:50 (estimated) – Dallas radio station KRLD reports that no arrests have been made, but police dragnets have been put out in downtown Dallas and the Oak Cliff neighborhood.

1:51 – Police Transcripts

Chief Curry – What are the circumstances of J.D. Tippit?

Dispatcher – We do not have it all clear yet, 1. He was involved in a shooting and was dead on arrival at Methodist and I am sorry that is all I have right now.

Curry – Did they get the suspects?

Dispatcher – We believe we have him in the Texas Theater now.

1:51- Police Transcripts

Dispatcher - Suspect in shooting of police office is apprehended and en route to the station…Caught him on lower floor of the theater after a fight.

(CE 2146) WFAA TV Reel, "Interview with Police Chief Jesse Curry," Nov. 23:

Q- Can you describe briefly what happened inside the theater?

Curry- Well, they were searching the theater and as they approached this man, he jumped up and said, "This is it," and drew a gun – attempted to draw a gun. They grappled with him and were able to twist the gun away from him and he was resisting violently. Several officers subdued him. I had two, two officers that had to have treatment for injuries wrestling around over the seats in the theater and another officer was scratched up but didn't have to have treatment."

1:55 – According to Detective Toney's report, at this time he and Lt. Cunningham are searching the balcony of the Texas Theater. They question a suspect who is not Oswald; the manager on duty says that this subject has been in the theater since 12:05 (long before the theater was open for business). The scuffle with Oswald occurs on the first floor of the theater at this time. It is interesting that so much anecdotal evidence places Oswald's capture at the theater closer to 2:00, yet the police transcripts have him arrested and on his way to City Hall as early as 1:51, placing the scuffle in the theater at least several minutes before that.

1:55 – Talbert – Your location?

Hill- Zangs and Colorado.

Talbert – You do have the suspect arrested in the Texas Theater?

Hill- Yes sir, him and the gun.

Hawkins – Captain Westbrook wants a photographer here at the Texas Theater.

Dispatcher – 509 is supposed to be en route.

"Note from J.W. to Jesse Curry of 23 December 1963": "Oswald was carrying, at the time of his arrest in the Texas Theater, a Smith and Wesson .38 caliber revolver, serial number 510210. This is the same caliber gun Officer Tippit was shot with when he stopped Oswald" (maryferrell.org).

1:55 – Sgt. Gerald Hill gets the call to go to the Texas Theater at this time, according to his report to Chief Curry (texashistory.unt.edu). The drive to the theater, the search of the theater, the scuffle and arrest all happen after this.

1:55-2:00 - *Life* gives this time ("almost 2:00") for Julia Postal's call to police. This is at least fifteen minutes later than her actual call according to police transcripts.

1:57 – KLIF reports on the radio that a Dallas police officer has been killed, "an independent tragedy...quite unrelated to the death of the president."

1:58 (CD 677) – Mrs. Kennedy and the casket containing President Kennedy leave Parkland Hospital, accompanied by SS Agents Kellerman, Hill, and Stout.

2:00 – Dallas Police Patrolman M.N. McDonald places his entry into the Texas Theater at this time. Once again, we have anecdotal evidence that Oswald's capture was at or around 2:00. McDonald does not say anything about Johnny Brewer pointing Oswald out to him. In this report, McDonald searches two suspects who are unarmed, before approaching Oswald and telling him to get on his feet. Oswald attempts to reach for the gun at his waist with his right hand. The two struggle for the gun and fall over, and other officers come to the rescue. As McDonald wrests the gun free from Oswald, he hears the hammer snap. By this time there are 7 or 8 officers surrounding McDonald and Oswald, including plainclothes detectives. Oswald is taken out of the theater (Letter to Chief Curry, Dec. 3, texashistory.unt.edu).

The plethora of anecdotal evidence placing the arrest at 2:00 or later raises a thorny question: Should we trust the police transcripts, placing the arrest before 1:51, or the recollections of all involved, placing it at 2:00? There is little evidence that the transcripts were altered in any way, and 1:50 is accepted by the Warren Report as the time of Oswald's arrest, so it remains mysterious why the arrest is so frequently placed at 2:00 in other reports.

2:00 – The *NY Times*, on Nov. 23, says "The arrest came about 90 minutes after the assassination" ("Police Relate Story of Swift Capture").

2:15 – The *NY Times* gives this as the time of the scuffle in the theater ("Leftist Accused, Nov. 22).

Regarding Oswald's arrest: In his Nov. 22 case report for Oswald's arrest for the murder of the President, Captain Fritz identifies all those involved.

Marion Baker: Saw Oswald in building after shooting.

Deputies Mooney and Weitzmann: Found rifle in TSBD, gave it to Fritz.

Fritz – Found empty and live shells used in offense.

Lt. Day – Lifted rifle used in offense, made prints from rifle and bag used to carry rifle.

Det. Studebaker – made investigation in TSBD.

Det. Hicks and Barnes – made paraffin tests of Oswald's face and hands.

Hill, McDonald, Walker, Hutson, Hawkins, Carroll: arrested Oswald

Mooney: Found *three* empty 6.5 rifle shells on 6th floor of TSBD

O.P. Wright (Parkland Hospital Security Officer) - Found 6.5 rifle slug, turned over to Secret Service at Parkland

Det. Johnson and Montgomery – Found paper at TSBD used to carry the rifle

Det. Graves – took affidavit from Helen Markham

Det. Senkel, Turner, and Potts – made search of 1026 N. Beckley

Det. Dhority – made lineup for McWatters and Whaley, identified bus transfer found in Oswald's pocket

C.W. Brown – made investigation at TSBD, took witnesses from TSBD to City Hall

G.F. Rose, R.S. Stovall, H.M Moore, J.P. Adamcik – made search of 2515 W. 5th st. in Irving; recovered blanket used to wrap the rifle; recovered Oswald's possessions; brought Wesley Frazier into City Hall for polygraph, found picture of Oswald holding rifle.

J.R. Leavelle- held lineup for Helen Markham, took affidavits of Callaway, Guinyard, Reid, Truly, Scoggins.

R.M. Sims – recovered bus transfer slip from Oswald's shirt pocket.

E.L. Boyd – recovered five live .38 rounds in Oswald's pocket

M.G. Hall – took affidavit from Lee Bowers

George Applin – saw Oswald come into picture show

In addition to the above, Fritz identifies several dozen other witnesses (texashistory.unt.edu).

3:15 - "Networks broadcast news of a suspect's arrest (Manchester).

3:23- "Networks identify Oswald by name; his age is given as 24" (Manchester).

3:26 – "Networks tell of Oswald's 1959 application for Russian citizenship; the public links Tippit's murder with the assassination" (Manchester).

4:09 – Police Transcripts *(Mary Ferrell Chronology)*

Deputy Chief Fisher- Has there been any developments that you can tell me about the shooting of the officer? Was there any connection with the shooting of the president?

Dispatcher – At this time it's my understanding it's the same person. He's in custody...That's not official. That's just the rumor up here.

Afterword: What Really Happened

The following is a more likely scenario than the one given to us by the Warren Commission. This is conjecture, but entirely based on the facts above.

At 12:30, when the motorcade was passing through Dealey Plaza, Oswald was on the 2nd floor getting the Coke, having eaten his lunch. Immediately after the shooting, he spoke with E.A. Reid, and then encountered Baker and Truly somewhere close to the entrance as he was leaving the building. He then gave Robert MacNeil directions to the payphone and left the building. Shortly after this, someone resembling Oswald (possibly accompanied by others) ran out of the TSBD and got into a Nash Rambler to leave the scene. Oswald walked to his usual bus stop, without arousing suspicion, and got on the bus heading toward his apartment (which would go through Dealey Plaza). He left the bus at 12:40 when it got stuck in traffic. He calmly walked to Whaley's taxi and asked for a ride. A woman approached the taxi, and not being in a hurry, he offered his taxi to her, and Whaley gave the ride to Oswald. Perhaps Oswald became concerned that he was being followed, but for some reason he asked to be dropped off five blocks south of his apartment.

Oswald walked to the apartment, changed his clothes, and saw Earlene Roberts, and she saw him put on the dark overshirt that she later referred to as a jacket. He was wearing this dark shirt over a white undershirt when he was arrested, and was never wearing the white jacket worn by the Tippit killer. While Oswald changed his clothes two police officers parked outside the house and honked. He ignored the police, but this must have rattled him. He grabbed his pistol, waited for the police to leave and went outside to wait for the bus (or maybe to consider his next move), with his transfer in his pocket. When the bus didn't come, he began walking to the Texas Theater, where he had been told to meet up with a contact. He didn't arouse the suspicions of the police because he did not resemble Tippit's shooter and was not leaving the Tippit shooting scene.

Meanwhile, someone unaffiliated with the Dallas PD told police that the suspect was 5'10", 30 years old, 165 pounds, and that he lived at 1026 N. Beckley. This happened no later than 12:43, thirteen minutes after the assassination. This person was a trusted, confidential police informant who had seen Oswald's 201 file, or was informed by someone within the CIA. The informant may have provided more information, even Oswald's name. Tippit was told to go find this suspect in Oak Cliff, and he searched desperately for him. Two officers went to Oswald's house but did not enter for some reason. Since information was compartmentalized in the police department, individual officers were not well-informed in the 90 minutes after the assassination, and they were receiving conflicting information in a piecemeal fashion. At around 1:08, Tippit, driving through Oak Cliff in search of Oswald, stumbled upon the man who killed him after a brief, friendly conversation. This man, or men, did not kill Tippit out of self-defense; this was an execution. Other police officers may not have known the true reason Tippit was in Oak Cliff.

At some point after 12:30 someone informed Johnny Brewer that he was to be on the lookout for a suspicious character who might be coming to the Texas Theater soon. He was probably shown a photo of Oswald and told that he was to inform the police as soon as this man arrived at the theater. He could've simply been told to be on the lookout for the man in the photo. Brewer could have been threatened; he was somehow made to understand the grave importance of this task. Perhaps he was told that this man was a suspect in the President's murder. Brewer may have recognized Oswald as a former customer of his shoe store. Brewer was necessary for obvious reasons: An informant could not be the one to alert authorities about Oswald's presence in the theater. Since this person would be an essential ingredient in an investigation, it had to be an innocent civilian.

Oswald entered the theater, possibly without paying, and sat on the first floor. He might have forgotten his meeting place in the balcony, or he might have chosen not to go there. He probably did not know whom he was supposed to meet and he had no idea that Tippit had been shot.

At some point someone other than Julia Postal (who only told police that someone entered the theater without paying, and didn't even know if he was still there) told police that the Tippit suspect was in the Texas Theater in the balcony. This could have happened much earlier, and the police would have known that a civilian would be making a confirmation when Oswald arrived. The police were sent there en masse, at the time that Brewer told Julia Postal to call the police. Some police may have arrived before 1:45, when the dispatcher first informed officers that a suspect had entered the Texas Theater. According to witness statements, the police were in the theater for about ten minutes, leaving with Oswald at 1:51. There are some reports that place the police entry time as early as 1:40. As the police carried Oswald out of the theater, a large crowd was chanting, "Kill him, kill him." Immediately following the arrest the Dallas Police Department assumed that Oswald had killed both Tippit and JFK, and they made this known to the public.

Made in the USA
Lexington, KY
26 March 2017